Resilience

Praise for *Resilience*

'I challenge anyone to read through it, highlight the lines that resonate and make sense, and then stand back and see what is left ... there won't be much.'

MARK EVANS MBE, FOUNDER, THE UNIVERSITY OF THE DESERT; EXECUTIVE DIRECTOR, OUTWARD BOUND OMAN; ROYAL GEOGRAPHICAL SOCIETY GEOGRAPHICAL AWARD WINNER.

'Highly readable wisdom travelling along the all-important road to resilience.'

DAVID STEPHEN, CHIEF RISK OFFICER, WESTPAC

'Essential for anyone who is interested in learning how to handle pressure or support other people who are facing challenging circumstances.'

RODERIC YAPP, LEADERSHIP FORCES

'A highly practical guide that takes you from setbacks to success. The advice rings true to experience.'

LEON TAYLOR OLYMPIC MEDALLIST, BBC COMMENTATOR; EXECUTIVE COACH

'This book has captured so many ideas that we can all learn from, to cope with any challenges that we are faced within life. We can choose to use these challenges to help us thrive and become stronger.'

WENDY CASSON, HEADTEACHER, EDUCATIONAL DIVERSITY, BLACKPOOL

'*Resilience* offers us practical wisdom, packaged in bite-sized chunks, to help us meet life's challenges with clarity, perspective and agency, and without depleting our emotional and physical energy.'

BAILLIE AARON, FOUNDER, SPARK INSIDE

Resilience

10 habits to thrive in life and work

JO OWEN

Harlow, England • London • New York • Boston • San Francisco • Toronto • Sydney
Dubai • Singapore • Hong Kong • Tokyo • Seoul • Taipei • New Delhi
Cape Town • São Paulo • Mexico City • Madrid • Amsterdam • Munich • Paris • Milan

PEARSON EDUCATION LIMITED
KAO Two
KAO Park
Harlow CM17 9SR
United Kingdom
Tel: +44 (0)1279 623623
Web: www.pearson.com/uk

First edition published 2020 (print and electronic)

ISBN: 978-1-292-28226-8 (print)
978-1-292-28227-5 (PDF)
978-1-292-28228-2 (ePub)

British Library Cataloguing-in-Publication Data
A catalogue record for the print edition is available from the British Library

Library of Congress Cataloging-in-Publication Data
A catalog record for the print edition is available from the Library of Congress

10 9 8 7 6 5 4 3 2 1
23 22 21 20 19

Cover design by Two Associates

Print edition typeset in 9.5/13pt and ITC Giovanni Std by SPi Global
Printed by Ashford Colour Press Ltd, Gosport

NOTE THAT ANY PAGE CROSS REFERENCES REFER TO THE PRINT EDITION

For Hiromi

The epitome of resilience in adversity

Contents

About the author

Jo Owen is the only person to win the Chartered Management Institute Gold Medal four times, for his writing on leadership. His books have been published in over 100 editions globally and he has featured in Fortune, the Financial Times, The Times, BBC and many magazines and papers. He has presented two television series on leadership.

Over the last twenty years he has conducted original leadership and resilience research with over 100 firms around the world. He has also researched extreme leadership with everyone from spies to sports people, from the Royal Marines and the nuclear deterrent to NGOs and start ups. He has gone to the ends of the world to research leadership in tribal societies from the Arctic to Australia, Mali to Mongolia, to Papua New Guinea and beyond. His resilience specific research has taken him from the advisory board of the Wellbeing Institute at Cambridge University, to Positive Psychology with the University of Pennsylvania and neuroscience at Harvard.

Jo practices what he preaches on leadership. He is the co-founder of Teach First, now the largest graduate recruiter in the UK. He has also started seven other NGOs with a combined turnover above $100 million. He was previously a partner at Accenture; he built a business in Japan and he started a bank. He started his career at P&G in brand management, where he put the blue speckle in Daz and became the best nappy salesman in Birmingham.

He is a keynote speaker at conferences on leadership, resilience, mindsets, global teams and tribal society.

Publisher's acknowledgements

005 Angus Deaton: Angus Deaton **008 Kogan Page:** Original interview with the author, first quoted in Mindset of Success, Kogan Page 2015 **013 Penguin Random House:** Jim Collins Good to Great. Random House 2001 **013 Wendy Casson:** Wendy Casson, Head Teacher Blackpool PRU **020 Arnold Palmer:** Arnold Palmer **030 Lady Caroline Lamb:** This was the description of 19th century romantic poet Lord Byron, by Lady Caroline Lamb. **034 William Shakespeare:** Othello, Act III scene 3. **037 Baillie Aaron:** Baillie Aaron: Founder and CEO of Spark Inside. **060 Cathy O'Dowd:** Cathy O'Dowd: first woman to climb Everest from both north and south sides **081 Andy Hertzfeld:** http://www.folklore.org/StoryView.py?project=Macintosh&story=Reality_Distortion_Field.txt&sortOrder=Sort+by+Date **082 HarperCollins:** Control Your Destiny or Someone Else Will (Collins Business Essentials) Paperback – 1 Apr 2005 by Noel M. Tichy and Stratford Sherman **086 William Shakespeare:** Hamlet V ii. **086 William Ernest Henley:** William Ernest Henley 1888 **089 Roderic Yapp:** Roderic Yapp, Royal Marine Commandos **106 William Shakespeare:** Claudius is speaking, in Hamlet Act IV scene V. **106 The Macmillan Company:** The Prince by Nicolo Machiavelli CHAPTER XVII Concerning Cruelty And Clemency, And Whether It Is Better To Be Loved Than Feared **106 William Shakespeare:** Hamlet **106 William Shakespeare:** Hamlet Act III Scene I **107 The King James Version:** Bible Galatians VI **107 Nick Clegg:** Nick Clegg: Deputy Prime Minister **109 The Macmillan Company:** Machiavelli The Prince Chapter XVII. **130 William Stukeley:** William Stukeley **135 William Shakespeare:** Hamlet III, Scene I. Part of the "to be or not to be" speech **135 HarperCollins:** FW Taylor, The Principles of Scientific Management (1911) ch 2, 59 **141 Tor Garnett:** Tor Garnett: Detective Superintendent, Metropolitan

Police **144 Le Petit Parisien:** Londres, Albert: Les frères Pélissier et leur camarade Ville abandonnent, Le Petit Parisien, 27 June 1924 **148 Hippocrates:** Hippocrates **160 Leon Taylor:** Leon Taylor: Olympic diving medallist **174 Hokusai Katsushika:** https://www.christies.com/features/Hokusai-7458-1.aspx. **174 Hokusai Katsushika:** Hokusai **177 Sean Parker:** Sean Parker has since left Facebook. This interview was first carried by Axios on November 9 2017, and widely reported across the media. https://www.axios.com/sean-parker-unloads-on-facebook-god-only-knows-what-its-doing-to-our-childrens-brains-1513306792-f855e7b4-4e99-4d60-8d51-2775559c2671.html **178 Penguin Random House:** Aristotle, 1941. The Basic Works of Aristotle, edited and with an Introduction by Richard McKeon, Random House, New York **179 Penguin Random House:** Aristotle, 1941. The Basic Works of Aristotle, edited and with an Introduction by Richard McKeon, Random House, New York **181 Unitarian Universalist Association:** Man's Search for Meaning. An Introduction to Logotherapy, Beacon Press, Boston, MA, 2006. ISBN 978-0-8070-1427-1 (Originally published in 1946) **184 FedEx:** https://www.youtube.com/watch?v=zyq06fuapD0 **185 David Stephen:** David was head of risk at RBS from 2013-18, and is now head of risk at another major bank. He had to sort out the mess resulting from the great financial crisis. **212 Simply Psychology:** The growth cycle is modelled in Kolb's learning cycle. Sims, Ronald R (1983). "Kolb's Experiential Learning Theory: A Framework for Assessing Person-Job Interaction". Academy of Management Review. 8: 501–508. Kolb was inspired by Kurt Lewin, the Gestalt psychotherapist. Kolb's four stages are: concrete learning, reflective observation, abstract conceptualization and active experimentation. Academics like long words. **212 Steve Jobs:** Steve Jobs **222 Viscount Leverhulme:** This remark is also attributed to US Department Store magnate John Wanamaker, to Henry Ford, to advertising entrepreneur and guru David Ogilvy and many others. See the WPP annual report 2013. http://sites.wpp.com/annualreports/2013/what-we-think/why-its-time-to-say-goodbye-to-ikthtmisoaiw/ **223 Mark Evans:** Mark Evans: explorer, founder of Outward Bound Oman **224 Kogan Page:** Author's original interview, first featured in Mindset of Success 2e, Kogan Page 2018 **225 David Sole:** David Sole **225**

The Metafit™ group: Royal Marines **238 John Wiley & Sons, Inc:** This is based on classic research. Herzberg, Frederick; Mausner, Bernard; Snyderman, Barbara B. (1959). The Motivation to Work (2nd ed.). New York: John Wiley. ISBN 0471373893. **239 Natasha Porter:** Natasha Porter, Founder and CEO of Unlocked **239 Crown Copyright:** From HMG prison and probation jobs website, retrieved 22/2/19. https://prisonandprobationjobs.gov.uk/prison-officer/tips-for-applying/ **241 Natasha Porter:** Natasha Porter, Founder and CEO of Unlocked

Resilience skills index

How you can put theory into practice

Think well, live well: the power of optimism

1. Cultivate an attitude of gratitude
2. Start the day well
3. Be smart in your choice of company, online and offline
4. Become the luckiest person alive
5. Become the colleague of choice

See light in the darkness: the power of emotional intelligence

6. Discover the value of negative emotions
7. Role-model positive emotions
8. Manage your emotions
9. Turn fear into courage

Be kind to yourself: the power of FAST thinking

10. Acquire fast, accurate, flexible and self-enhancing thinking
11. Identify your iceberg beliefs
12. Challenge your iceberg beliefs: make them work for you
13. Identify your mind traps
14. Cope with your mind traps

Control your destiny: the power of self-belief

15. Build mastery
16. Deal with setbacks: watch the movie, not the snapshot
17. Build your influence

Reach out: the power of connections and networks

18. Build trust
19. Listen effectively
20. Practise appreciative constructive responding
21. Gratitude: hunt the good stuff
22. Network with purpose

Recharge your batteries: the power of recovery

23. Take rest breaks
24. Reduce your working day
25. Ensure your work is focused and efficient
26. Use the power of recovery and rest
27. Sleep your way to success
28. Diet realistically, diet for life
29. Exercise to perform, not compete
30. Manage your energy flows: the energy grid

Stay mindful: the power of choice

31. Breathe to take control and focus
32. Visualise to prepare for success
33. Slow down external events: buy time and create space to find a smart way forward
34. Create options: avoid getting stuck in a binary win–lose, find creative solutions

Craft your mission: the power of purpose

Keep on learning: the power of growth

Find your sanctuary: the power of culture

Introduction

Feel good, function well: the power of resilience

Every day we face minor irritations such as traffic jams and queues. Some people react well, others react poorly: the same event produces different reactions in different people. You probably react differently on different days to the same irritation: some days a queue can be a chance to use your smart phone, while on another day the irritation produces annoyance. The critical insight is that you always have a choice about how to react to events. You are not a victim of events where each event inevitably produces a certain reaction. This is true not just of minor events, but also of major life events and career events.

If you can choose how to react to events, it pays to choose well. The essence of resilience is learning to make good choices in real time.

"You always have a choice about how to react to events."

Most of the time, the choices you make about how to react are instinctive. You will have developed habits of mind which enable you to navigate life easily day to day. All of these habits of mind are so deep we do not even realise that we have them. Just as you do not have to think about how to breathe, so you do not have to think about how to react to many daily events. Most of these habits of mind will serve you very well. But there may be some that trip you up at vital moments. Being able to identify those reactions that help you and hinder you is a vital first step to building habits of mind which will make you even more resilient in the future.

Resilience is not a single skill, like playing the piano. It is a series of habits of mind that you can learn. Everyone has countless habits of mind and developing them is, literally, the work of a lifetime. The research shows that there are ten types of mind habits which are most important for building resilience.

The magic of resilience is that you do not need to work on all ten habits to feel good and function well. If you focus on just one habit, that can make a huge difference. For instance, as a recovering pessimist, I found that learning the power of optimism has been transformational. You can decide which habit of mind you want to focus on first. You can choose your own path to resilience. This book outlines 45 practical skills and actions to help you navigate your path easily and successfully. Although this book is deeply rooted in research, it is also intended to be highly practical.

"You can choose your own path to resilience."

The ten main habits of mind which build resilience are:

1. **Think well, live well: the power of optimism.** Optimists live longer and better than pessimists, and they also perform better at work. The good news is that optimism can be learned. Simple exercises can help you: noting the good things that happened during the day, managing your social media habits well and learning how to react positively to new ideas and situations. The chapter on this habit evens shows how you can learn to be lucky.
2. **See light in the darkness: the power of emotional intelligence.** Even negative emotions have value if you know how to put them to use. Emotional self-regulation is vital to resilience to help you deal with adversity and fear. This chapter shows how you can manage your fears and build your courage to deal with difficult situations.

3. **Be kind to yourself: the power of FAST thinking.** Resilience often happens in the moment: instinctive reactions take over and we either act resiliently or do not. Often our internal chatter is less than helpful and we can be our own worst critics. This chapter shows how you can control your internal chatter. This allows you to make informed and better choices about how to react in the moment.
4. **Control your destiny: the power of self-belief.** In good times it is easy to have self-belief. The real test is whether you can sustain self-belief in adversity. This chapter shows how you can react to setbacks positively and effectively, and how you can learn from each setback to become more resilient and more effective in future.
5. **Reach out: the power of connections and networks.** Resilience is not about enduring life alone. By reaching out problems can be halved and joys can be doubled. Reaching out is not a transaction: it is about building relationships and influence in the good times to sustain you in hard times. Simple and practical exercises will help you deepen your relationships at work and at home.
6. **Recharge your batteries: the power of recovery.** It is impossible to sustain high energy and high performance for ever. Even the best athletes need structured rest periods. Modern work blurs the distinction between work and home, which means it is easy to never switch off completely. This chapter shows how you can regain control of your time so that you can work better by working smarter, not longer.
7. **Stay mindful: the power of choice.** This chapter is about managing the 1% of your time which is the high adrenaline, make or break moments of your career. Resilience is not just about managing adversity and persevering for the long haul. It is also about making the right choices in real time and turning crises into opportunity.
8. **Craft your mission: the power of purpose.** If your mission is to climb Everest or win a competition, it is easy to feel a strong sense of purpose. Having purpose gives you the strength and

resilience to overcome setbacks. This chapter shows how anyone, even people with apparently mundane work, can craft their jobs so that they have a real sense of purpose which allows them to flourish in what they do.

9. **Keep on learning: the power of growth.** The skills that help you succeed today are not the skills that will help you succeed in ten or twenty years. You need a mindset which is open to continually growing and learning. But learning new skills takes effort and is risky: it means trying new things which rarely work the first time you try them. This chapter shows how you can turn the random walk of experience into a structured journey of discovery which will sustain you throughout your career.
10. **Find your sanctuary: the power of culture.** Most people adapt to the standards and the culture around them at work and at home. It pays to find a culture where you can flourish. This matters not just for where you live and work, but also for how you interact with the social media. This chapter shows how the choices you make can affect you and those around you at home and work.

"The skills that help you succeed today are not the skills that will help you succeed in ten or twenty years."

The resilience challenge

Imagine what you would do in each of these real events:

- **Scene 1:** You have two seconds in which to prove that 20 years' hard work has been worthwhile. You are standing at the top of a ten-metre diving board, getting ready for an acrobatic dive with your partner. 15,000 people are watching you live, plus the judges, millions of people on television and your mum. You either win the Olympic medal or do not. You have no second chances. It is all or nothing.

- **Scene 2:** You are a female high-flying graduate. You are working with some of the most dangerous and violent people in the country as a prison officer. On an early shift, one of the male prisoners decides to 'pot' you: he empties a large pot of three prisoners' urine over your head. Meanwhile, a colleague is dealing with a suicide in a neighbouring cell.
- **Scene 3:** Your colleagues are actively trying to get rid of you. Everything you do is being examined in minute detail by the media. The right-wing media hate you because you stop the government being right wing. The left-wing media hate you because you prop up a coalition government led by a right-wing party. You have to keep going under this pressure for five more years as Deputy Prime Minister.

The heroes of each scene not only coped. They came out of each experience stronger. The lessons they learned in extremity apply to anyone in day-to-day life. Each scene illustrates the three sorts of resilience that you need day to day, although perhaps not in such extreme circumstances:

- **Scene 1: the planned crisis.** You may not jump off the high board, but you may have to present to the board, or perhaps you have to make a pitch to a big client or negotiate with a major supplier. These are all moments of intense pressure where you have to be at your best to succeed. Like the high dive, you may not have a second chance.
- **Scene 2: the unplanned crisis.** In any organisation there is a limitless supply of crises and conflicts. Events and people may conspire against you, and you have to find a way through it fast. You need to be able to react well in the moment.
- **Scene 3: sustained pressure.** Your career is a marathon, not a sprint. You have to sustain your energy, optimism and performance for decades, not just for days.

The research for this book found that it is possible not only to cope with such challenges, but to thrive from such challenges. The secret is not in your DNA. The secret is about how you think. We all have habits of mind: some help you and some hinder you.

The good news is that the people who feel good and function well have consistent habits of mind which anyone can learn. That is the purpose of this book. It will help you discover and build the habits of mind which will do more than let you cope with crises and pressure. They are habits of mind which will let you thrive.

Resilience is about helping you feel good and function well.

About this book

There is now a huge body of research around resilience, but remarkably little of it is based on the world of work. The most compelling research has been in education and the armed forces, where you have groups of people who can be subjected to programmes and tests in a systematic way. The messy world of work has been largely ignored. The purpose of *Resilience* is to address that omission: it looks explicitly at why resilience matters at work, and how you can build your resilience.

Resilience is a response to a growing need at work. The old certainties and restrictions of twentieth-century firms are being replaced with greater freedom, uncertainty and ambiguity in the twenty-first-century. You can no longer rely on your employer for long-term employment: you have to rely on your own employability. With greater freedom comes greater responsibility, greater risk and greater opportunity.

> **"You can no longer rely on your employer for long-term employment: you have to rely on your own employability."**

Surviving and thriving in this new world requires deep resilience, not only to overcome short-term adversity but also to sustain long-term high performance. Resilience is not just about endurance and survival: it is about learning to flourish.

Resilience origins and credentials

Resilience came about from the intersection of two of my passions.

My first passion has been leadership, where I attempt to practise what I preach. I have been researching leadership for over 20 years and have written 20 books on leadership and management. I have also started eight social enterprises with a turnover of over $100 million annually, including Teach First which is the largest graduate recruiter in the UK. I have started a bank and have been a partner in various firms. As ever, practice is a humbling antidote to theory.

My exploration of leadership soon found that the best leaders are rarely the most skilled leaders. The good news is that no leader gets ticks in all the boxes: you do not need to be perfect to succeed. The best leaders all have something extra: they act differently because they think differently. At the heart of how they think differently is the idea of resilience. Often, the difference between failure and success is as simple as giving up.

"The best leaders are rarely the most skilled leaders."

My work on leadership pulled me inevitably towards resilience. The pull was strengthened by observing just how much more stressful work has become for everyone as a result of the increased uncertainty and ambiguity of the world of work.

My second passion has been education. As with the world of work, it has long been obvious that the most successful children are the most resilient. Even before resilience became a fashionable topic of research the evidence was there, albeit disguised. For instance, of the big five personality traits,[1] the only one consistently associated with academic success is conscientiousness,[2] which is a vital part of resilience.

As ever, it pays to put theory into practice. As chair of a resilience charity, I have been able to see what happens when you put a structured resilience programme into schools. In a fully randomised control trial funded by the Education Endowment Fund, it has produced stellar results in raising resilience. We are due to hear the results on academic achievement soon.

My work on leadership and education made it impossible to avoid dealing with the challenge of resilience.

This book draws on over 20 years of original research I have been conducting on leadership. I have also conducted extensive original research and interviews for this book. Ten of the most striking interviews I conducted now appear in the book, each one highlighting one of the habits of resilience. These 'portraits of resilience' are deliberately gender-balanced. If all the portraits were of male mountaineers and sportspeople it would give a completely unbalanced perspective on the nature of resilience.

In addition to the original research, I have been fortunate to complete programmes with the University of Pennsylvania on positive psychology and with Harvard University on neuroscience[3] to gain a better understanding of some of the science behind resilience. The book also draws explicitly on the research in this area, and is referenced accordingly.

The reality is that resilience is a work in progress because the research continues and our understanding of it keeps on growing. This book attempts to explore the state of the art as it is today.

How to use this book

You can read this book in at least three different ways:

- You can read the book conventionally from start to end. You will find the book flows naturally from personal habits of mind, such as optimism, to more career-focused habits and actions such as growth and finding your sanctuary.
- You can read the chapters in any order you want. If you want to discover the art of managing your energy in the short and long term, you can start with Chapter 6. A good way to find out which chapters you want to focus on is to use the index at the start, and then check the short introduction at the opening of each chapter.

- Finally, you can speed-read the book. Each chapter follows the same simple-to-follow format. It starts with a brief introduction which tells you what the chapter will deliver, and ends with a summary of the key learning and action points. Reading the start and end of each chapter will give you a quick idea of where you will want to focus.

However you use the book, you will find plenty of practical exercises in each chapter, backed up by case histories, interviews and research which you can explore as much as you want.

As you read this book, you will find many themes, such as optimism and choice, that keep on recurring. That is the nature of resilience. It is not a single skill like learning to type. It is a series of linked skills which all support and reinforce each other. To make reading easy, each skill is treated independently so that you can focus on it properly.

Inevitably, there is an argument about how many skills make up resilience. Some of the skills are very closely related: locus of control and self-efficacy are close relations and I have tied them together under the banner of self-belief. Pulling in the other direction, optimism can be dissected into a much wider set of skills. This meant that some simplification has been required. I have identified 45 leading skills and actions which you can take, and condensed them into 10 themes which are meant to be mutually exclusive but collectively exhaustive. Wherever you want to dive deeper into a topic, I provide nearly 200 references for you to pursue.

Acknowledgements

One of the key ideas of resilience is that you cannot flourish alone. Writing this book gave me ample proof of that message. This book would not have been possible without the support and encouragement of many people who have been more than generous in their personal and professional support for this effort.

Some truly exceptional people shared their experiences of resilience in the worlds of sport, expeditions, business, government, charities and entrepreneurship. In all, I have interviewed over a thousand people in more than a hundred organisations: my thanks to them all and I hope they got as much out of the process as I did. In particular, I would like to thank those who have agreed to be featured in this book including: Wendy Casson, Nick Clegg, Mark Evans, Sumayyah Hassam, Cathy O'Dowd, Tor Garnett, Natasha Porter, David Stephen, Leon Taylor and Roderic Yapp. The interviews were gender-balanced because resilience is not just a male topic.

I also want to pay tribute to Emma Judge who is not just a leading thinker and trainer of resilience, but has also demonstrated huge resilence. She puts theory into practice.

I have been fortunate to have had, once again, great support from my publishers at Pearson. Richard Stagg has been a source of insight and help for more years than I care to count, and Eloise Cook has once again proven her worth as my editor. There is also a vast team in the background who quietly make it happen, including Antje King and Felicity Baines. I am also forever indebted to my agent, Frances Kelly, who saves me from contractual work so I can focus on writing.

Finally, I am in awe of one person to whom I owe a lifetime debt: my wife Hiromi. She not only provided huge support when needed, but she has been a role model of resilience in very difficult circumstances. I have learned so much from her.

If, despite all this support, there are still errors and omissions, then only I can be held responsible.

Chapter

Think well, live well: the power of optimism

Optimism is a matter of life and death. Put simply, optimists live longer and live better. Optimism is not inherited: anyone can learn to be more optimistic. As a recovering pessimist, this is very good news. This chapter will show:

- Optimists live longer
- Optimists live better
- What optimism really is, and is not
- How anyone can become more optimistic

Optimists live longer

Nuns show just how much optimism matters if you want to survive.[4] Nuns are very good for such research because most of the control variables have been removed: they have similar beliefs, they have the same daily routines, the same diet and the same access to medical care. We could say that they have the same habits.

678 nuns of the School Sisters of Notre Dame agreed to take part in a study. 180 had written autobiographies on entry into the convent, at an average age of 22. The purpose of the autobiographies was to identify the educational needs and interests of the novices, and any emotional language was purely coincidental. Researchers realised that the emotional language could be useful. They carefully coded the words used by the nuns. Words expressing joy, hope, gratitude, happiness, interest and love were all positive. Words expressing anxiety, shame, confusion, fear or sadness were negative.

To make this simple, we can regard the nuns with the positive autobiographies as the fun nuns: they positively wanted to become nuns. The nuns with the negative emotions we can call the duty nuns: they were doing what they thought they ought to do.

So what happened to the nuns nearly six decades later? At age 80, the mortality rate for the duty nuns was three times higher than the mortality rates for the fun nuns.[5] The fun nuns were alive and having fun while the duty nuns were dead or in ill health. Feeling good is a key survival technique, at least for nuns.

Nuns may be an unusual, although useful, sample. But what happens if we look at the population as a whole? It is possible to find good data on mortality from atherosclerotic heart disease (AHD). Typically, AHD is linked to physical conditions and lifestyle: obesity, smoking, diabetes and hypertension are all good predictors of AHD.

But it turns out that even if you combine all the traditional predictors of AHD, they are not as good as one other predictor of AHD: how you speak. How you speak predicts your likelihood of suffering from heart disease.[6]

"How you speak predicts your likelihood of suffering from heart disease."

Psychologist Johannes Eichstaedt[7] reviewed the use of language in Twitter at county level across the US. Twitter language is the best predictor of AHD: it has about 40% predictive power, whereas the seven most important traditional predictors of AHD only muster 36% predictive power between them.[8]

The Twitter language which will kill you is highly negative, combining hostility and hatred (f**k, f**king, bitch, shit, a***hole, hate) with boredom and fatigue (tired, sleep, bored, soooo). The language which might just keep you alive is optimistic (opportunity, goal, strength) and about positive experiences (great, friends, food, weekend).

Living in a county of optimism and positive experiences is better for your health than living in a county of hatred or boredom. Language is a powerful symptom of much wider and deeper challenges that many of the hatred and boredom communities face. If all the people around you express hatred and boredom, you are likely to get infected with that view of the world. The language and experience of where you live may determine your life prospects.

It turns out that optimism can also predict health and longevity at national level as well as county level.

For the first time in decades, life expectancy has stopped rising and is even starting to fall back. Nobel-Prize winning economist Angus Deaton noted that morbidity among middle-aged white Americans is rising significantly.[9] If morbidity had continued to decline at the same rate as it did from 1979 to 1998, then over 500,000 deaths would have been avoided from 1999 to 2013: that is far worse than the AIDS epidemic. So what was going on? Deaton clearly points the finger at the 'diseases of despair' which include opioid-heroin overdoses, alcoholism and suicide. The current era of angry politics reflect and reinforce these diseases of despair, which is not good for a nation's health.

Looking at a broad cross-section of the community, Harvard researcher Eric Kim analysed morbidity and optimism among 70,000 women between 2004 and 2012.[10] He found that the most optimistic (top quartile) women had 30% less risk of dying than the least optimistic (bottom quartile). There is no surprise to find that the most optimistic women are less at risk from coronary disease and stroke: these diseases are often linked to stress. More surprising was to find that the optimists were also less likely to die from cancer (16%) or from infections (52% less likely).

So why would optimists be less likely to die from problems such as infections, which appear to have nothing to do with optimism? The key lies in an idea closely linked to optimism: self-efficacy. Self-efficacy is sufficiently important to merit its own chapter in this book, Chapter 4. If you are optimistic you will believe that you can control your destiny, whereas, if you are pessimistic you will believe that your destiny is out of your hands. Optimists do not hope to get lucky: they make themselves lucky. The optimists believe it is worth taking precautions to avoid getting disease and injury. If they need treatment, they will then follow through with the medication and remedial treatments. Pessimists will not be so proactive or diligent.

"Optimists do not hope to get lucky: they make themselves lucky."

Optimism can even boost your immune system. A study[11] of immunity to influenza vaccine in elderly individuals showed that the optimists had an enhanced response to the vaccine. The optimists were also more likely to take exercise and have a lifestyle which was kind to their immune system. As with other optimists, they have a sense of self-efficacy which means that they take care of themselves. Optimism can save your life.

By now, this research was becoming mildly catastrophic for a lifelong pessimist. But it was about to get worse: I soon discovered that the optimists not only live longer, they live better and perform better than pessimists.

"Optimism can save your life."

Optimists perform better

MetLife, the US insurance firm, had a challenge. It hired over 5,000 life insurance people every year, but lost 80% of them within five years. 50% of them left within one year. That is a huge churn at a huge cost: it costs a lot to find and hire each new salesperson, and it costs even more to train them up. MetLife estimated it was wasting $250 million on making poor hires, and losing even more on missed sales. Put positively, taking on this challenge could reap big rewards for MetLife.

Step forward Professor Martin Seligman of the University of Pennsylvania.[12] He believed there was an opportunity. Instead of hiring to aptitude, MetLife should hire to attitude. It is easier to train aptitude (skills) than it is to train attitude (beliefs). He reasoned that people with a positive mindset would do better than people with a negative mindset. To test his theory, he tested all potential hires for optimism. He then persuaded MetLife to hire the most optimistic people who had only just failed the aptitude test: these people would normally be rejected by MetLife.

"It is easier to train aptitude (skills) than it is to train attitude (beliefs)."

These optimistic rejects went on to outsell their more skilled but less optimistic colleagues by 21% in their first year. As they became more skilled in their jobs, they went on to outsell their less optimistic peers by 57%. This research has been replicated many times in other industries from real estate to forestry products.

There are at least three reasons why optimists outperform:

- **Optimists have self-efficacy:** They believe they can succeed. This is the same reason why optimists have better health. If you believe you can control your destiny, you take steps to ensure a good outcome. So the optimists are more likely to be ready to learn and change in order to succeed, whereas the pessimists may avoid taking risks and will stick to a tried and trusted formula, even if it is not the best.
- **Customers prefer to deal with optimists:** On a visit to a school, I asked a class if they had ever been taught by an unhappy teacher. A forest of hands went up. The children knew when they had an unhappy teacher, and they all hated it. We all know when we have a miserable teacher, boss or colleague. It is infectious. In contrast, an optimistic and positive colleague is normally a joy to work with.
- **Optimists have resilience:** They bounce back from rejection better than pessimists who can take it personally and catastrophise. For instance, Mike Tobin was a successful CEO of a growing data centre business. He started his career selling kitchenware door to door. It is gruelling work. You can expect to succeed at only 1 or 2 doors in every 100. That is a 98% rejection rate. How would you cope with the door shutting in your face 98 times out of 100?

> His reaction was simple: "Every time a door shut in my face, I knew I was one door closer to success."[13] Optimists keep going because they think about the world differently.

At least in the world of sales it is easy to measure performance. But most managers live in a highly ambiguous world where it is hard to measure individual performance. For instance, if you are asked to prepare a report, it could be anything from 1 page to 100 pages long. However long it is, there will always be another fact to gather, another opinion to canvas. Unlike a sale, there is no point at which a report can be complete until the deadline arrives. It is even harder to measure performance across managers: Sharon's client may have been delighted and Adil's may have been disappointed, but that may be comparing apples and oranges, or even apples and bicycles. How do you adjust for the challenge of each project, the support and resources available and the nature of each client?

Nevertheless, the available research shows that optimistic managers can induce better performance. Optimistic managers do a better job of supporting and engaging their team: an engaged team and manager do much better than a disengaged team. Research by Greenberg and Arakawa[14] showed that workers in the bottom quartile of engagement scored an average of 11/20 on projects, while the most engaged team members (top quartile) scored 17/20. That is the difference between barely surviving and flourishing.

The critical takeaway from this research is that an optimistic and engaged team depends on you as a manager. One study found that 65% of staff would prefer a new boss to a pay rise.[15] If you are a manager, then your beliefs and behaviour have a big impact on the behaviour, attitudes and performance of your team. If you do not like the attitude of your team, look in the mirror. If you like their attitude, look in the mirror and pat yourself on your back.

The final piece of the jigsaw is that optimists are likely to get richer, even if they are not so well respected. Investment is a never-ending battle between the bulls and the bears, between the optimists and the pessimists. Over time, the optimists win. The bears will see all the risks: they see a wall of worry while the optimists see a mountain of opportunity. The pessimists stay out of the market, while the optimists dive in. But over any ten-year period stocks beat cash 91% of the time.[16] Warren Buffet, the legendary investor and one of the richest people on the planet, is famously optimistic. Every year for the last 40 years he has produced an investment letter: analysis shows that in 35 out of 40 he has been positive about the future. Where others saw risk, he saw reward.[17]

> **"Optimists are likely to get richer."**

This optimism is not easy to sustain. We tend to be risk-averse and loss-averse: memory of losing money in the great banking crash of 2008–9 is painful and more salient than all the small gains since then. The small gains add up to a fourfold increase in the S&P in ten years.[18] Nobel-Prize winner Daniel Kahneman[19] noted that we all use shortcuts, or heuristics, to make decisions. These are very useful for day-to-day thinking, but these shortcuts all have biases which are not always helpful. Loss aversion is a bias which does not help if you want to invest. Inevitably, there will be another crash before or after publication of this book. It will be a moment for the pessimists to savour and to say: "I told you so." Meanwhile, the optimists will quietly reinvest amid the carnage and get rich slowly again. History is on their side.

Optimists seem to have it all because they:

- live longer
- perform better at work
- become richer.

Before exploring how to become functionally more optimistic, it pays to understand what optimism is and what it is not.

What optimism is and what it is not

We all recognise optimistic people when we see them. They seem to live in the sun, not under a cloud. But defining optimism is harder. Before attempting to define optimism, here are three perspectives to help you think about it.

- Is optimism extrinsic or intrinsic?
- Is optimism about being happy all the time?
- Is optimism about hoping to get lucky?

Is optimism extrinsic or intrinsic?

The hotel receptionist was clearly having a bad day. She avoided any eye contact. While she checked me in she was having a tense phone conversation with a guest. Finally, she threw my key card across the counter and as she did so her corporate training kicked in and she barked out: "Have a nice day." What she clearly meant to add was "... and please drop dead." I felt for the receptionist. We all have those moments, when we really are not enjoying what we do. It is hard to function well at such moments.

Being positive and optimistic is not something that can be imposed from outside. It is not about muttering some stock phrases as if they are magical chants which will make people feel good and function well.

> **"Optimism comes from within you: it cannot be imposed on you."**

Being positive and optimistic comes from within. Finding your intrinsic motivation matters for you and for the people you work with. This is a challenge that STIR[20] addresses head on. The UN estimates that there are 750 million children who are in school, but not learning. The heart of the problem is with disengaged teachers who either do not turn up to school, or who are present but not committed. This problem is also a huge opportunity: if you can help these teachers rediscover their intrinsic motivation, you can change the lives of 750 million children.

Traditionally, governments have focused on the extrinsic motivation of teachers: carrots and sticks. In some countries, teachers are highly paid, while in others, teachers have to clock in and out using biometrics to ensure they cannot cheat. Neither the carrots nor the sticks have much effect. STIR has taken the opposite approach: it works with governments to help teachers and officials rediscover the intrinsic motivation which brought them into teaching in the first place.

STIR has shown that when professionals are given autonomy and support, and they achieve even greater skills mastery, their intrinsic motivation rises. This is reflected in improved teacher attendance and improved pupil performance. The extrinsic motivators of carrots and sticks are far less effective than enabling teachers to rediscover their intrinsic motivation through autonomy, mastery and support.

Optimism comes from within you: it cannot be imposed on you.

Is optimism about being happy all the time?

It is neither possible nor desirable to be happy all the time. There are times we will not be at our best. Bereavement, illness, loss of jobs and other setbacks are all part of life. We may want to learn to dance in the rain, but we should not dance on the ashes of our loved ones. As we shall see in Chapter 2, negative emotions are important and can help build our resilience, if you manage them well.

"It is neither possible nor desirable to be happy all the time."

There is a deeper risk of seeking happiness all the time. The risk comes in the form of the hedonic treadmill: we always want more. Back in 1943, Abraham Maslow wrote a famous paper which gave rise to Maslow's hierarchy of needs.[21] He argued that at minimum, we all need food, water and shelter. Once we have that we want to be safe physically and economically, then we want a sense of belonging. Once we have that we want esteem from our community and then we want self-actualisation where we fulfil our dreams.

The problem is that our dreams have no bounds: we graduate from wanting a bicycle for Christmas, to buying a second-hand car, to getting a fancy car, and then eventually we buy our own jet before dreaming of our own space programme. To make it worse, we are always comparing ourselves with our peer group, which means there is always someone who seems to have more and to do better. In Maslow's words, we are "needs junkies: whatever we crave, we always crave more". This hedonic treadmill is a treadmill to nowhere.

To see the danger of the hedonic treadmill, think of your parents or grandparents: the chances are that they were no more or less happy than you. Now think of going back to their time: try living without computers, mobile phones, internet, Google or social media. Could you be happy?

"We are 'needs junkies: whatever we crave, we always crave more'."

Would you swap your life with that of a prince or princess 300 years ago? At first, the idea of being royalty appeals. But now get rid of electricity, heating, running water, indoor toilets, sanitation, antibiotics, dental care, painkillers and cappuccino machines. You would live your life in fear of death by some vile pre-industrial disease, or murder by a rival.

Happiness, like optimism and resilience, is not a function of your external environment. Do not let the world dictate to you how you should feel. All these things come from within you, it is natural that sometimes you will feel positive and sometimes negative. You cannot avoid these ups and downs, but you can learn to manage them well to build your resilience, as we will see in Chapter 2.

Is optimism about hoping to get lucky?

I first discovered that hoping to get lucky is a dangerous form of optimism when my good friend Giancarlo drove at speed through some red lights and across four lanes of heavy traffic. As I recovered my breath, I asked why he had jumped the red lights. "Red lights," he replied "are lights which are wanting to go green." Giancarlo's impressive optimism is not a good recipe for longevity, nor is it a good recipe for managerial success.

Hoping to get lucky can be dangerous in more subtle ways. Research on American prisoners of war in Vietnam showed that hoping to get lucky was not a good survival strategy. The most senior prisoner, Vice Admiral James Stockdale, noted that some prisoners started with hope: they hoped they might be out by Christmas, Easter, Independence Day or Thanksgiving. As each landmark came and went, so their hope slowly dried up. In his words, they eventually died of a broken heart.[22] The survivors were ready to face the brutal facts and then deal with them. Unfounded optimism can lead to hopelessness. Effective optimism is linked to an ability to see the brutal facts as they are, and to deal with them.

> "Effective optimism is linked to an ability to see the brutal facts."

Hoping to get lucky is fine if you buy a lottery ticket, which gives you permission to dream. Hoping to get lucky as a manager does not work because luck is not a method and hope is not a strategy. As with the Vietnam PoWs, your optimism as a manager has to be linked to an ability to see the brutal truth and deal with it. Optimists do not run away from reality or from challenge: they lean into it.

> "Luck is not a method and hope is not a strategy."

Portraits of resilience: optimism

Wendy Casson, Headteacher, Blackpool Pupil Referral Unit

Wendy Casson came bouncing into the room, full of energy. A child had just thrown a can of baked beans at her. Wendy had ducked in time and was looking forward to welcoming the child back into her school the next day.

Where others saw a problem child, she saw a child with problems. Where others gave up, she made it her mission to give hope to the child. She had to accept children from mainstream schools where the schools had given up on teaching them. Wendy ran the largest Pupil Referral Unit (PRU) in the UK: it is the place where rejected children go. Top policy-makers have been happy to dismiss PRUs as scrapheaps or preparatory schools for prisons. If you run the country's largest PRU, you need deep resilience.

The children in the PRU often faced multiple and horrendous problems. One child had suffered abuse, and her abuser was her carer. Another was deemed to be psychotic and could go from 0 to 90 miles an hour in a millisecond: he was always on edge. A third had discovered the joys of drugs, another was self-harming and children with poor homes, poor parenting, poor diet and poor behaviour were commonplace.

Wendy saw through all of this: "We have some beautiful young people here. There are only a few we cannot find the key to." She talked about the boy who had just thrown the can of beans at her: "I saw a little lost boy with no boundaries and no parenting ... all I know is that the child has been let down, so it makes you more determined to help."

What keeps her going is a passionate belief in making a difference, about changing the path of these young people. Where others see problems, she sees opportunity.

Wendy's optimism is baked in reality. She does not hope to get lucky: she faces the brutal facts and brutal reality of dealing with children who have chaotic lives. Her optimism is supported by a high degree of self-efficacy (see Chapter 4). She has no doubt she can make a difference – it is also supported by high aspirations and a strong sense of purpose (see Chapter 8) and by a strong team (see Chapter 5). As we shall see, resilience is rarely based on just one strength. Deep resilience comes from different strengths reinforcing each other.

Learning optimism: the power of feeling well

In the cult movie *Flash Gordon*, the evil emperor Ming[23] orders all his subjects to rejoice, on pain of death. The corporate world tends to follow this example by demanding passion, enthusiasm and commitment until you are fired.

We know we cannot be told to be happy or passionate, because those feelings come from inside us. If happiness cannot be imposed on you, can anger and negative emotions be imposed on you? Imagine you have had a long and difficult day. At the end of it, a colleague you do not care for comes up to you and starts to push all your buttons. You suspect your colleague is deliberately trying to annoy you. You have every right to feel angry, annoyed and upset. But there is no law that says you have to feel angry, annoyed and upset. That is your personal choice.

The first step towards learning optimism is to realise that you always have a choice about how you feel.

You do not need to be a victim of the world where all your emotions are dictated to you by events, colleagues and bosses. They may push you in a certain direction, but only you can choose whether you go there or not.

"You always have a choice about how you feel."

Understanding that you always have the power to choose your feelings is the vital first step. Once you know you can choose, you can start to choose well. As someone who was brought up to believe that the only reason it is not raining is because it is about to rain, this was an astonishing and liberating discovery. Once you know you have a choice, you are free to choose well.

At first, it is hard to believe that our feelings are not hard-wired to our conditions. If external conditions control our outlook on life, we would expect lottery winners to be among the happiest people on the planet. A study of major lottery winners showed that this is not the case.[24] Fairly quickly, lottery winners get used to their new-found wealth, which becomes their new normal. This has the effect of reducing the pleasure they find from mundane events: it takes something special to make them happy. Overall, they appear no more happy than a control group of people who do not play the lottery. It seems that money really cannot buy you happiness.

At the other end of the scale, incarceration clearly does lead to loss of wellbeing, but only for the time that prisoners are inside serving their sentences.[25] On release, their happiness bounces back and they take great pleasure in the mundane benefits of freedom, which lottery winners miss. It appears that ex-prisoners can be as content as lottery winners.

The first vital step to learning optimism is to know that you can learn it. How you feel is how you choose to feel and how you think is how you choose to think. This is easy to say, but hard to do. We all have habits of mind which we have acquired over the years. As with any habit, it is hard to unlearn an old habit and to learn a new one. It helps to have some routines and exercises which will enable you to develop optimism, not pessimism.

Here are four simple exercises to help you develop an optimistic frame of mind.

Exercise 1: cultivate an attitude of gratitude

Sit back and reflect on all the bad stuff that has happened today. Think about all the bad news on television, delays getting into work, annoying emails, boring meetings ...

On second thoughts, do not do this exercise. It is a good way to feel bad.

Let's start the exercise again. This time think of all the good things that happened today, from the moment you woke up in a warm bed in a safe country. When I ask groups to do this exercise, they quickly come up with a very long list, even when I ask them to focus on just the first five minutes of the day. We take the mundane benefits of modern life for granted. Rediscovering the basic joys of modern life is a good way to influence your mood positively.

You can repeat this exercise at any time of the day in a couple of moments as you walk to or from the coffee machine. It is a simple way to reset your mindset. The most powerful time to do this exercise is at the end of the day. This is the time when it is easy to start ruminating about what has happened and worrying about what might happen tomorrow. Rumination and worry are the perfect recipe for losing sleep.

Instead of ruminating, reflect on what went well in the day. Find just three things to be grateful for, professionally or personally. Then write them down. If you want to log them on a computer, do so the next day: avoid screens and social media at the end of the day. Writing it down is essential: it consolidates your thinking and commits it to memory. As your log of things to be grateful for expands, you start to discover just how much you can be grateful for. People who do this report a significant and sustained improvement in their wellbeing. Alternatives to logging three good things are to log three things you have learned, or three ways in which you have helped others or made a difference. These are all simple ways of focusing on what is good in your life from day to day.

In the short term, this exercise helps you sleep well and feel good. Over time, it lets you cultivate an attitude of gratitude: it helps you frame a positive outlook on life. Your default view will not be to focus on problems and setbacks, but to reflect on what is good. When you know what you appreciate and want, you can manage your life towards having more of what you want.

Exercise 2: start the day well

If you want a good day, start it well. The good news is that most people are creatures of habit first thing in the morning. Your choice of routine is also a choice about how you want to face the day. It is worth making it a deliberate choice, not a default choice.

The goal of this exercise is to cultivate an attitude of gratitude: find three things you can be grateful for first thing in the morning. This could be as simple as waking up to your favourite music instead of waking up to the news. Or it can be about noticing and being grateful for the many minor miracles of modern life which we now take for granted (see the following case example).

Whether you start the day with a smile or a scowl, you are likely to continue that way. Build your routine so that you start by noticing what is good about your life. There is plenty to be grateful for and plenty to enjoy.

How to wake up in the morning

It had been a hard research trip in the middle of the African bush. I got back to a hotel with a corrugated iron roof and a barbed wire fence. I slumped asleep in a filthy bed. The next morning, I awoke to two miracles in two minutes. First, I went to the bathroom and turned on a tap: cold running water came out. I did not need to walk two kilometres to draw water from a crocodile-infested river. Then I turned another tap: warm water came out. I did not need to gather firewood to heat the water.

I had been used to getting up in the middle of wars, famine, disasters, lying politicians and shifty business leaders. It is called waking up to the news, and it is not a good way to start the day. Now I start every day with two miracles in two minutes: hot and cold running water. From there on I start to notice all the other mundane miracles of modern life. It is hard to have a bad day after that, although I still succeed sometimes.

Although we can all choose how we feel, some choices are easier than others. The Twitter analysis of counties across the US pointed to the existence of whole communities of anger, despair and ill health. You can still choose to be positive and optimistic in such a context, but it is not an easy choice. If you live in a community of optimism and positive experiences, it is easier to be positive and optimistic.

It may be hard to move from your physical community, but you can choose your online community, so choose carefully. The evidence of the effects of social media is wildly split between studies which show that it is the devil incarnate and those that show that it is the engine of wellbeing.

There is an impressive list of studies that point to the challenges of social media which can lead to the following:

- Low self-esteem,[26] especially where we compare our lives and bodies with those of others.
- Depression,[27] where we feel we are wasting our time on social media.

- Anxiety.[28] Users of seven or more social media platforms had significantly higher anxiety than the average population. It is not clear which way causality flows: does anxiety drive greater social platform usage or vice versa?
- Addiction.[29] Sean Parker, the founding President of Facebook, was clear that they set out to hack the human brain.[30] He succeeded. Social media is more addictive than alcohol or nicotine. Each new like or view of one of our photos or Tweets gives us another little hit of dopamine. The brain always craves more dopamine, so the incentive to keep on for another hit from social media is strong. Social media turns us into dopamine junkies.
- Violence and extremism. A UNESCO report[31] found that the social media echo chamber can be a platform for spreading and reinforcing extreme and fringe views, leading to radicalisation and violence.

"Social media turns us into dopamine junkies."

This is a far cry from the original vision of social media which was a glue to keep existing social networks together, and to help people extend their social networks. The difference between the two extremes appears to be in how you use social media. Heavy usage, the constant search for approval from strangers, and living in an echo chamber of negative views is a good way to find the devil incarnate in social media. Used lightly as a reinforcement and extension of positive social networks, it can be a force for good.

Exercise 3: be smart in your choice of company, online and offline

This is a simple exercise. Do a stock-take of your professional and personal worlds. Do you tend to feel positive and optimistic when you engage with them, or negative, cynical and angry? In the words of Roman poet Aesop: "You know a (wo)man by the company (s)he keeps." Choose your company well.

I have interviewed thousands of senior executives, and nearly all of them admit that luck paid a significant factor in their rise to the top. Then they quickly add: "But of course, you have to make your own luck." How can you learn to be lucky?

Richard Wiseman,[32] a professor at Hertfordshire University, set out to research luck. He came across an incredibly lucky woman who was always winning holidays, money and cars. She did not even drive, but she kept on winning cars. How can anyone be so lucky? Part of the answer came from discovering that she entered over a hundred competitions a week. Luck was her full-time occupation. She exhibited two of the three vital factors which can make you into the luckiest person alive: persistence and practice. The third luck factor is perspective. Persistence, practice and perspective are the three Ps of luck.

"Persistence, practice and perspective are the three Ps of luck."

Persistence

History is full of heroes who were serial failures before they succeeded. Abraham Lincoln was an outstanding failure before he became President. He lost seven elections, had two failed businesses, which left him with debts that took seventeen years to pay off, and then after the death of his fiancée he had a nervous breakdown and stayed in bed for six months. But he kept going. Ultimately, the difference between failure and success is as simple as the difference between giving up and keeping going.

Practice

A comment attributed to legendary golfer Arnold Palmer[33] is "the harder I practise, the luckier I get". This is true. The novice might hole a ten-foot putt one in ten times, but with practice they might succeed two in ten times. A seasoned professional will probably succeed eight times out of ten. So is the successful putt a lucky putt or a skilled putt? The more the lucky woman entered competitions, the more practice she had at completing tie breakers such as, "Say in 12 words or fewer why Sudso is wonderful ..."

The essence of good practice is not just persistence: it is focused and deliberate practice. Stay focused on getting lucky (or skilled) at one thing, not many. Know what you want to be great at, be it golf, entering competitions or financial analysis. Deliberate practice is about active learning: always push your limits, get help, coaching and support. After ten years, you want to have had ten years' experience, not the same one year of experience repeated ten times.

Perspective

This takes us straight back to exercise one above. In many ways we are as lucky as we feel we are. We can count our blessings or we can count our curses: your choice determines just how lucky you believe you are. To be born in an era of relative peace and great prosperity is a huge blessing. Would you really swap your life for that of any of your ancestors?

You also need perspective to spot your opportunity. Many of the great businesses of today have been built on the back of a lucky break or an obvious opportunity. Microsoft was born when IBM was looking for an operating system for its new PC: Bill Gates duly obliged. Google is built on the obvious business model of paid search. Facebook was built to connect friends at university. Although these opportunities are obvious now, they were not obvious at the time. It took both imagination and courage to seize the opportunity. The billionaires of tomorrow are seizing opportunities today which you or I cannot yet see, but which will seem obvious to us in ten years. Make the next obvious opportunity your opportunity.

Exercise 4: become the luckiest person alive

If you want to be lucky, apply the three Ps of luck:

1. Persistence. Failure is as simple as giving up. The more you persist the more likely you are to find some luck.

2. Practice. Skill is often mistaken for luck, especially by the less skilled. The harder you practise, the better you become.
3. Perspective. Reflect positively on your day, year and life and you will discover huge amounts of luck to be grateful for. And if you look for opportunities in the right places you can create your own luck in the future.

"You will be remembered not for what you do, but for how you are."

There are plenty of colleagues and leaders you have to follow, and a few you may want to follow. No one wants to work with a cynical and negative colleague. If you want to be the leader people want to follow, not have to follow, it pays to be positive and optimistic.

At work, being optimistic is not about hoping to get lucky: it is about believing you can make the future better. As a colleague and a leader you will be remembered the same way that you remember other colleagues. You will be remembered not for what you do, but for how you are. You do not need a bowl of sweets by your desk to be remembered well. You need to exhibit consistently positive and constructive behaviours. Five simple behaviours will ensure you are seen as a positive, constructive and optimistic colleague and leader.

Offer solutions, not problems

The good news is that there are always problems to be solved in every team. If there were no problems, there would be no need for management. Some people are very good at delegating problems upwards to management or down to their team. So it is a huge relief to everyone when someone has the courage to offer a solution, not a problem. If you are the person with the solution, you find that you quickly assume control and become the person other people follow. You become the leader. And if your first solution does not work, make sure you have Plan B in reserve.

Step up, not back

Every team has moments of crisis when no one is sure what to do. It is easy to step back, or to point the finger of blame or indulge in displacement activity like analysing events and holding meetings. None of this achieves anything. The positive response is to look forward, not back. Drive to action: this means acting on what you can control and not worrying about what you cannot control.

Listen actively

The best leaders are like the best salespeople: they have two ears and one mouth. And they use them in that proportion. In a time-starved world, listening is a powerful form of flattery. It tells the speaker that you value their wisdom so much that you want to invest your time in listening to them. Instead of offering smart answers, ask smart questions which help you find out what you need to find out. Only when you understand the other person's position fully can you persuade them of your position: if you ask the right questions, they will persuade themselves for you. Listening is a very positive and effective way of persuading.[34]

Respond positively

People and firms are risk averse. When new ideas arise in a meeting it is common to see everyone launch heat-seeking missiles at the new idea: risks and problems will be explored, probing questions will be asked. At the end of the inquisition, the idea will be dead and everyone will have learned that there is no point in offering ideas. Instead of this usual response, enforce a routine of looking at the benefits of an idea before exploring the concerns. Placing benefits before concerns respects the idea and its originator. It also means that good ideas do not get crushed at birth, and it encourages other ideas to surface. Putting benefits before concerns is a simple way of being positive and constructive.

Say thank you

When someone helps you or does something well, take time to thank them: it costs nothing. To make it really count, let them relish the moment by exploring the success with them. Ask how they achieved it, and express how it helped you. You are not wasting time: you are investing in a relationship.

> **"Listening is a very positive and effective way of persuading."**

Exercise 5: become the colleague of choice

Becoming the colleague of choice is about how you are, as well as what you do. Here are five ways you can be the colleague or boss that people want to work for, rather than the one they have to work for:

1. Offer solutions, not problems.
2. Step up, not back at moments of crisis and uncertainty.
3. Listen actively to influence, persuade and flatter.
4. Respond positively to ideas and help.
5. Say thank you.

If you can apply these disciplines consistently you will be well ahead of most of your colleagues: you will become the colleague of choice.

Summary

Optimism and positive thinking are core components of resilience. Evidence also shows that if you are optimistic and positive you will:

- live longer
- perform better at work
- become richer.

The good news is that you can learn optimism and positive thinking. You can choose how you feel and behave. Do not let others impose their feelings on you. Simple exercises to help you become more optimistic include:

- Recall three good things at the start and end of the day (and any other times). Write them down at the end of the day.

- Start the day well. Avoid the news and focus on what you can be grateful for. Start the day with an attitude of gratitude.
- Manage your world. Choose your social media activity carefully. Find a professional and social environment which is positive and optimistic.
- Learn to get lucky. Most leaders admit that they got lucky, but that they made their luck through a combination of persistence (sticking at it) and focused and deliberate practice (becoming talented at something).
- Offer solutions not problems. Respond to ideas by exploring their benefits before concerns: seek the good stuff before looking at the risks.

As leaders, you cannot tell your team to be positive and optimistic, but you can create the conditions in which they will make that choice. In particular, you can be the role model for the team to follow: no one wants to work for an unhappy, cynical and pessimistic boss.

Chapter
2

See light in the darkness: the power of emotional intelligence

Both positive and negative emotions can help you at work, and this chapter shows how. Instead of running away from negative emotions, learn how they can help you. Even anger, fear and embarrassment can work for you.

This chapter also shows how you can build positive emotions for yourself and for your team.

An in-depth case shows how you can turn fear into courage. You can acquire the courage to take on new challenges, difficult tasks and step up when others choose to step back.

Why it matters: deal with negative emotions

If you were offered a life free of all pain, would you accept the offer?

There are a small number of people who already have a life free of all pain. They have a rare disorder known, unsurprisingly, as congenital insensitivity to pain (CIP).[35] This sounds like a blessing: no need to fear the dentist's needle and drill, no pain from stubbing your toe or falling over and no need to resort to opioids to control your pain.

Feeling no pain is a curse, not a blessing, for people with the condition. Professor Geoff Woods of the University of Cambridge[36] started to study this condition after coming across a boy in

Pakistan who felt no pain. The boy earned money in street theatre by doing extreme and painful things like walking on hot coals and sticking daggers in his arm. Before Woods was able to examine the boy, the boy had jumped off a roof to amuse his friends. He felt no pain from the injuries he sustained which eventually killed him. Lack of pain is a fatal curse.

In practice, pain serves a very useful purpose: it is a warning signal to us that something is not right. If we feel no pain from putting our hand in boiling water, then we will not learn to avoid boiling water. Many of the people who have CIP have short lives, and they are often regarded as retarded: they keep on doing clumsy and dangerous things and appear not to learn from their mistakes. Learning can be painful, and lack of pain means lack of learning about danger.

Having declined the offer of a life free of pain, here is another offer for you. Would you like a life free of negative emotions? With one wave of a magic wand you can say goodbye to fear, envy, greed, regret, anger, grief, embarrassment and anxiety. Like the pain-free life, this offer sounds too good to pass up. Like the pain offer, this is a blessing which is likely to be a curse in real life. Like pain, negative emotions have a positive purpose in helping us navigate life well.

"Negative emotions have a positive purpose."

Lack of emotions, or simply very shallow emotions, are the hallmark of a psychopath. They feel little guilt or remorse, are very low on empathy and are not inhibited by fear or anxiety. They are happy to pursue their own interests at any cost to others, take any risk that may hurt them or others and will feel fine about doing so. They are "mad, bad and dangerous to know".[37] They are especially unpleasant if they are one of your colleagues or, worse, your boss. Unfortunately, psychopaths can be very successful. Up to 3 to 4% of senior management may be psychopaths:[38] their boldness takes them to the top, even if they destroy people, careers and businesses on the way.

Lack of negative emotion is harmful, but too much negative emotion is also harmful. Negative emotions are labelled 'negative' for good reason: they are emotions which can do immense harm if they become permanent or strong. For instance, if you are permanently anxious, it becomes hard to make decisions, step up to deal with crises and conflicts or to deal with difficult people and situations. It is hard to be a highly anxious and highly effective manager.

Managing your emotions is a pre-condition of resilience. If your life and work is dominated by negative emotions you will struggle to survive long in the workplace. But if you never have any negative emotions you will also struggle to survive. The key is to achieve an elusive balance of negative and positive emotions. As a first step, it is worth recognising the surprising value of negative emotions. We will then explore how you can manage them to achieve balance.

"Managing your emotions is a pre-condition of resilience."

For a moment, review the list of negative emotions below and decide for yourself if anything can be positive about these negative emotions:

- anger
- anxiety
- boredom
- confusion
- embarrassment
- fear
- jealousy
- pessimism
- regret.

A good way to discover the importance of these emotions is to ask yourself what would the world be like, and what would you be like, without this emotion. It quickly becomes clear that in context and in proportion, each of these negative emotions has a useful purpose. Like physical pain, they are a call to action and a call to change. Let's look at each in turn, briefly.

Anger

An angry world is clearly dangerous, but what about a world with no anger? The civil rights movement was built on a bedrock of anger against the obvious injustices of the 1950s. Anger against real or perceived injustice is the classic call to action and call for change. This anger can be positive or negative: one side's freedom fighter is the other side's terrorist. And anger does not have to be violent: from Gandhi to Mandela to the Suffragettes and Extinction Rebellion there are plenty of examples of anger at injustice being expressed peacefully and succeeding, even in the face of violence against their peaceful protests. You can feel angry and use that as motivation, without having to express anger externally: in the workplace, this is the best way to channel your anger.

Anxiety

Anxiety and diligence walk hand in hand. If you are never anxious about anything, you probably never care enough to prepare properly, to do a good job and to push yourself. Too much anxiety about a big presentation will freeze you with fear, whereas a little anxiety ensures you prepare carefully. No anxiety probably means poor preparation leading to regret later.

Boredom

Boredom is useful and dangerous. Boredom happens when you are in easy street, living life in your comfort zone and not stretching yourself. This is also when you can recover and recharge your batteries. If you lived a life with no boredom, where you were in a state of perpetual frenzy, you would soon burn out. Phases of boredom are fine. But if you become continually bored at work, that is a sign that you are not progressing: you need to stretch, challenge yourself and get out of your comfort zone. Boredom is particularly dangerous for CEOs. Bored CEOs are the ones who start dreaming about the great takeover or brilliant new idea which will make, or more likely break, their firm.

Confusion

How can confusion be good? There are people who exhibit no confusion: they have complete faith that they are always right about everything. At their best they can be inspirational. In practice, they are often painful to work with because they do not listen, and they are incapable of learning, adapting and changing their minds. This can lead to disaster: they have a completely fixed mindset and view of the world. Confusion is an appropriate response to an ambiguous and uncertain situation: it shows that you need to step back, observe, think and adapt.

Embarrassment

Embarrassment is a highly effective form of social control, in both personal and professional settings. When we break a social norm, we are embarrassed. When no one feels any embarrassment, social norms adjust to standards which previously would have been unacceptable. Parents, still dressed in their pyjamas, taking their kids to school or going shopping is a classic example. In years gone by, it would have been far too embarrassing to act that way. Now, the old social norm is being challenged by people who have no embarrassment acting that way. At work, social norms also dictate dress codes, which are highly tribal: top management and front-line staff dress differently and IT coders and sales have their own dress codes. Dress the wrong way and you feel awkward. More importantly, this peer group pressure is very strong in forcing behavioural norms. You not only have to follow your tribe's dress code, you have to follow its behaviour code, which may or may not be what is written in the employee handbook.

An embarrassing journey

The Tokyo subway is a miracle in many ways. But the biggest miracle of all are the passengers. The busier the crowds become, the more well behaved they become. Each train stops at exactly the same spot on the platform: markings are painted on the platform to show where each set of doors will stop. Passengers form two orderly queues at the point where the train doors will open. As the train stops and the doors open, both queues take two steps forward and one step to the side, to let the arriving passengers out of the train. Once they have disembarked, the two queues move forward and on to the train.

> As a *gaijin*, or foreigner, there is an obvious chance to apply *gaijin* rules if you are in a rush: sneak in at the front of the queue to make sure you get the first train. Do this, and no one will say anything so you can get away with it. But then you feel like a complete idiot who has just confirmed to the Japanese that all foreigners are indeed uncivilised and badly mannered.
>
> I can confirm that total embarrassment follows and you learn never to apply *gaijin* rules again. Embarrassment is a highly effective form of behaviour control.

Fear

Fear is vital to survival. If you do not fear the oncoming tiger or car, you may not live to regret it because you may not live. Fearlessness wins soldiers many bravery medals, many of which are awarded posthumously. But if you fear everything, you can achieve nothing: you probably would not even venture outside home for fear of all the dangers of the outside world. As with all negative emotions, fear is useful in proportion and in the right context.

Jealousy

In Shakespeare's *Othello*, Iago warns: "Beware, my lord, of jealousy! It is the green-eyed monster which doth mock the meat it feeds on."[39] Inevitably, the green-eyed monster takes over and tragedy ensues. Jealousy can be highly destructive. But if we never felt any jealousy of anyone else, we would either be a saint, or we would be happy always to settle for second best. Jealousy is the product of a competitive spirit: if we are jealous of a colleague receiving a promotion, pay rise or bonus, that should stir us to raise our game.

"Fear is vital to survival."

Pessimism

Chapter 1 was devoted to the power of optimism. So let's hear a (small) cheer for pessimism. Pessimism is the long-term version of fear: it is about recognising and dealing with threats which may emerge in the future. As one Jewish friend put it to me: "My family used to be divided between optimists and pessimists. Today, we are all pessimists. In the 1930s, the pessimists saw the dangers and fled Nazi Germany, the optimists thought it would be fine. They stayed and perished."

Pessimists will say that they are simply realists who prepare appropriately against risk. As ever, it is a question of balance. If we all were complete pessimists, we would probably all be living like survivalists in bunkers in the wilderness. But if we had no pessimism, we would not take out insurance, we would not bother to secure our house, we would not save for a rainy day and we would not even carry an umbrella for the rainy day.

Regret

Regret seems utterly pointless: why cry over spilt milk, because the event has happened? You cannot change the past. But regret helps in two ways. As with all memories, regret is not about recording the past but about preparing for the future. Regret about the past helps us learn about how to do better in the future. And the prospect of regret is a powerful incentive to act well: the prospect of regret may stop us drinking too much, it may encourage us to use a contraceptive and take our medicines. It also encourages us to work well: we do not want the regret of facing the consequences of failure. Feeling regret about the past and the prospect of future regret are spurs to acting well.

> **"Regret is not about recording the past but about preparing for the future."**

Exercise 6: discover the value of negative emotions

The goal of this exercise is to help you put your negative emotions to work for you. Review the following table which summarises how negative emotions can help, and how their absence can hinder. This is not an invitation to wallow in negative emotions, but it is an invitation to help you make the most of your emotions. Awareness is the gateway to choice. As long as you are aware of your emotions, and aware of how you can use them, you can choose to put them to productive use.

Negative emotion	**Benefit**	**Absence of emotion**
Anger	Call to action	No challenge to injustice; exploitation of groups/individuals
Anxiety	Makes you focus on a problem to solve	No preparation for tough times
Boredom	Opportunity to recharge batteries, often our most creative time	Burn out through hyper-activity
Confusion	Forces problem solving	Over-confidence
Embarrassment	Build social intelligence	No social norms
Fear	React to, avoid danger	Dangerous behaviour
Jealousy	Spur to working better, harder	Acceptance of second best
Pessimism	Raises awareness of threats	Unready for known dangers
Regret	Encourages learning	Never learn, reckless behaviour

There are many more negative emotions to list, such as guilt, sadness and grief. This is not the place for an encyclopaedia of negativity. You can use the table above as a spur to working out how any negative emotion you encounter can be of value to you. And you may want to take some time now to identify other negative emotions you feel from time to time, and how they might help you.

Portraits of resilience: emotions

Baillie Aaron, Founder of Spark Inside

It is fashionable to talk of leaders needing to admit to vulnerability and weakness. Baillie is recognised as a strong and visionary CEO. Both she and the organisation she founded to bring coaching into prisons, Spark Inside, have received multiple awards for their work. Baillie is also one of the few leaders who has the courage and self-awareness to actually talk about the doubts and demons she has faced.

The problem started when Baillie hired a team member who performed well at interview, but whose attitude changed for the worse after a while in post. This individual's negative impact was particularly hard for Baillie: "Somehow they found my vulnerable spots and rather than supporting me, they gained pleasure from sticking the knife in. Despite being the CEO, I felt that I was being bullied." During this period, Baillie started doubting her own vision and her leadership ability. As Baillie put it, this was an 'existential crisis'. If you doubt your own life's work, you have a problem. It led to a "downward spiral of self-confidence, which made me a worse leader with less belief in myself or my vision". She also found it hard to seek help, and did not know how to ask.

Eventually, with the support of her family, friends and colleagues, Baillie took hold of the situation. She had built a highly supportive network without realising it: they saw her need and stepped up. Reaching out (see Chapter 5) made all the difference. She also managed her energy (Chapter 6) by sleeping more and by focusing more on her outside life which is completely different from her work life: her dancing demands balance and gave her balance. Rediscovering her purpose (Chapter 8) and vision helped Baillie greatly.

Reflecting on events, Baillie said: "Sometimes you choose the challenge, sometimes the challenge chooses you. But I got to the heart of my weaknesses and now I know how to respond and come through. I have strengthened my vision and become a better leader as a result of this experience." That is a hallmark of true resilience: to gain strength from adversity.

Why it matters: build positive emotions at work

Most of us prefer to live with positive, not negative, emotions. This is true both at work and at home. A core theme of this book is that you can choose how you feel. Knowing that you can choose your feelings liberates you from being the victim of events and colleagues. If you choose your emotions well, not only will your performance improve but the performance of your team will also improve.

If you come into the office with your little cloud of gloom, you will soon find it spreads like a major depression across your whole team. If you come with optimism, hope and a strong sense of self-efficacy, your team is likely to follow you. Your emotions can help your team's performance:

- Interest in work encourages creativity and problem-solving.
- Gratitude to your team builds their confidence and self-esteem.
- Self-efficacy encourages a can-do spirit and drive to action.
- Optimism supports self-efficacy and enables the team to see and take opportunities.
- Pride in the task underpins high standards and commitment.
- Security, not threat, encourages experimentation and innovation.

> **"The simplest way to deal with negative emotions is to drown them out with positive emotions."**

These are all emotions which you can cultivate in yourself and your team by setting the right example. The more you build these emotions, the less space there is for negative emotions to emerge. The simplest way to deal with negative emotions is to drown them out with positive emotions. However, uncontrolled positive emotions and a complete absence of negative emotions is not just unrealistic, it is also dangerous. Just as negative emotions have benefits (see the table in Exercise 6), so positive emotions can have a dark side (see the following table).

Positive emotion	Benefit	Danger
Self-efficacy	Can-do spirit and drive to action	Tilting at windmills
Optimism	See and take opportunities	Blind to risks and challenges
Security	Safe to experiment and innovate	Distraction from core task
Gratitude	Builds confidence and self-esteem	Complacency
Interest	Curiosity and creativity	Lack of action focus: 'analysis paralysis'
Pride	Commitment to doing a good job	Inflexibility, lack of growth or learning

You can build these positive emotions for yourself. We have already seen how you can build optimism and gratitude through the simple act of writing down three good things at the end of each day. You can use the same exercise to build pride and self-efficacy by noting the things you have achieved or done well. Interest and a sense of security come from finding a role and a place where you will flourish. You are accountable for your own career, so you have to ensure that where you work works for you. You can find out more about how to do this in Chapter 10: Find your sanctuary.

Exercise 7: role-model positive emotions

You can set the emotional tone for your team. Start by deciding what tone you want to achieve. The next vital step is to role-model those emotions, which means you have to be true to yourself. This means finding the best of who you are, then focusing on that: dial up your strengths and dial down your weaknesses. The following table shows some simple ways you can build the emotional tone of your team.

Positive emotion	Benefit	Team leader actions
Self-efficacy	Can-do spirit and drive to action	Break complex tasks into simple steps Be clear about what you want Delegate well
Optimism	See and take opportunities	Be an optimistic role model Explore the benefits of ideas before exploring the risks
Security	Safe to experiment and innovate	Show you care about each team member, their career and their future
Gratitude	Builds confidence and self-esteem	Focus on frequent, positive feedback
Interest	Curiosity and creativity	Encourage team debriefs and learning Be open to problems as well as solutions
Pride	Commitment to doing a good job	Set and keep high expectations

The good news is that there is no magic in setting the emotional tone for your team. The bad news is that you have to be 100% consistent. If you keep on changing the rules of the game, your team will find it hard to read you. Confusion will set in and morale will droop. So the emotional tone should not be a wish list of perfect traits you want to see in your team; it has to reflect the sorts of habits which you can sustain and role-model month after month.

Setting the emotional tone: the dark side of being positive

The CEO of the bank had a great speech, which he used often. It was based on "Don't bring me problems, bring me solutions!" It always worked. It sounded positive and action-focused. But it had a dark side. It meant that everyone was in fear of mentioning problems to him.

As the economy weakened, the bank's loan book slowly fell apart. No one dared to tell the boss: he wanted solutions, not problems. Eventually, the problems could not be covered up any more and the bank had to be bailed out. It cost over $100 billion of taxpayers' money.

He fell into the trap of all autocrats and dictators. They never want to hear anything that contradicts the story they tell themselves of being the hero of unending success. So they are told what they want to hear, not what they need to hear. They never see the danger until it is too late.

Take care in how you set the emotional tone of your team.

Building positive emotions for yourself and your team does not come about by accident. It requires awareness of your choices. As with all habits of mind, learning the habits requires deliberate choice and conscious practice to start with. Eventually, it becomes second nature as the new habits displace the old habits.

Cultivate the habit of managing your emotions: principles

Buddhist monks spend a lifetime devoted to the art of breathing as the gateway to controlling their minds and finding enlightenment. If you are an accountant faced with completing the month-end close, you do not have the luxury of learning how to breathe for years. You need a quick way of learning how to control the rising sense of panic and frustration that you may miss the deadline.

Exercise 8: manage your emotions

The three-step approach below is a life hack: it is imperfect, but it works. For most of us, that is what matters. We do not need to be experts, or to find enlightenment. We need a simple approach which will work for us most of the time. The three steps are very simple:

- How?
- Why?
- What?

This is known, originally, as the 'How why what' model. Here is how it works.

1. How do I feel, right now? This seems a really stupid question, but it is not. Most of the time we do not question how we feel – we just feel. But awareness is the gateway to choice and control. If we are never aware of how we feel, we just drift out of control. Once you are aware, you can choose whether you want to feel that way or not. So, if you are feeling focused, inquisitive and engaged, you can keep going. But if you are bored or angry, you can choose to do something about it. You cannot control your feelings unless you are aware of them.
2. Why do I feel that way? This is a good opportunity to vent. Think of all the external factors that drive you to think negatively. If someone you dislike has deliberately tried to upset you, you have every right to feel angry and annoyed. But there is no law that says you must be angry and annoyed: that is your choice.
3. What do I want to do about it? You can choose to stay with your negative emotion. If you are bored, you might want to stay that way: it is a good chance to recover and do something mindless like watch a TV soap opera.

The principle is easy to state, and easy to put into practice once you are familiar with it. To help put it into practice, we will look at a practical example of how you can turn fear into courage at work.

Cultivate the habit in practice: turn fear into courage

Turning fear into courage is one practical example of how even the deepest emotions can be learned through habit. Fear and courage are vital: they kept our ancestors alive in the past and keep your career on track today. If our ancestors had no fear of what was behind the bush, they might be eaten by a lion. Fear fuels survival. But it also stops us achieving our full potential. If you are to succeed, you need to take risks in order to:

- learn new skills
- take on new tasks
- step up when others step back
- have difficult conversations
- manage conflict.

This leaves you with a delicate balancing act. Fear helps survival but inhibits success, while courage helps your success but may lead to failure. Put it another way:

- Fear = survival ≠ success.
- Courage = success ≠ survival.

Some years ago, I led a group that was discussing fear, courage and the mindsets of the best leaders. They saw that most mindsets are simply habits of mind which can be learned, like optimism or self-efficacy. And then the topic of courage came up. A senior member of the local government team folded his arms across his chest and declared: "Well, courage is simple: you either have it or you don't. You can't train courage!"

I looked around the room in some alarm. Everyone was waiting for the brilliant insight about how you can train courage. But I had no idea if you could train courage or not. At the back of the room I saw the local fire chief, so I turned to him and asked how he trained his firemen to be so brave.

The local fire chief stood up. I saw him as the fifth cavalry charging over the horizon to save me. "The first thing I want everyone to know is ... I never want to have a brave fireman! A brave fireman becomes a dead fireman fast, and that is no use to me."

I was crestfallen. So I asked him how he got firemen to do things that mere mortals think are dangerous, like climbing tall ladders to go into smoke-filled, burning buildings. The fire chief beamed happily and explained how he could get anyone to do such things. You start by learning how to put on some basic kit and clothing, how to climb a small ladder safely and how to put out a fire in a pan. Slowly, the kit becomes more sophisticated, the ladders become longer and the fires become more hazardous and complicated. Eventually, you will be doing things that anyone else thinks is highly courageous.

The Royal Marine Commandos have exactly the same approach, albeit far more intense and more extreme. They start with simple, basic drills and slowly work up towards some of the toughest exercises anyone can imagine. The lesson from both the Marines and the fire service is that courage can be learned in small steps, which makes the abnormal feel normal.

"Courage can be learned in small steps, which makes the abnormal feel normal."

As a manager, you can learn courage the same way as firemen and Marines: one step at a time. This is about learning routines and habits that make the unfamiliar become familiar. For instance, every manager is a salesperson. The more senior you become, the more your job becomes selling: you have to sell your ideas and priorities to sceptical bosses, competing peers and indifferent customers. So how do you learn to sell? One small step at a time. Ideally, your first pitch is not to the CEO and board of your business. In practice, you will have had plenty of experience of selling already: you will have been selling your ideas to friends, family and immediate colleagues quite naturally as part of your everyday life. All you need to do is to focus on growing this experience in a deliberate manner.

Learning to sell

Sales is hard but rewarding: you know exactly how well you have or have not performed every day, and you get immediate feedback on your performance in real time from your clients who either buy or do not buy.

I learned to sell washing powder in the north of Scotland, and I learned the traditional way. I spent days following an experienced hand. After each call, I would ask endless questions about why he did or did not do things. Eventually, he let me do some of the preparation for some of the calls. Then he let me lead on part of the call. And finally, he let me lead some calls under his close supervision: they were all calls on old friends of his who he knew would behave. And they were small stores, so success or failure was not vital. I was learning in small steps.

Eventually, he let me loose on a store all by myself. The store manager took one look at me and asked if I wanted a bunch of fives. I had not heard this expression before, but his clenched fist (the bunch of five fingers) and his shouting gave me some idea of what he meant. From there it was but a small step to becoming the best nappy salesman in Birmingham, after which my career has been all downhill. You can learn from failure and success. All learning involves some risk.

Courage is mostly about learning routines and habits that make difficult and dangerous tasks seem easy and safe. This is the extrinsic approach to learning courage: learn the routine and what appears to be courageous to others is business as usual to you. But why is it so hard to learn new routines?

Watch any toddler and they are very keen to learn how to walk, even though they keep on falling over all the time. That does not stop them – they pick themselves up and have another go. That is how young children learn: through a process of endless trial and error. Success is the product of endless failure. But then, at some point, we learn that we should not fail. We learn to be fearful and we lose the courage to try. Fear of failure is drilled into us throughout school: failing tests and failing exams is to fail as a person. Then we reach work, and we learn that failure is bad for your career. Instead of being praised for making an effort, trying something new, we are more likely to be blamed for the wrong outcome. This makes us all deeply risk-averse at work.

"Success is the product of endless failure."

Learned fear sits on top of the congenital fear which has been passed down to us by our ancestors as a key to survival. Our genes, our schools and our workplace all tell us that we should fear taking risk and fear making mistakes. But if we had always feared making a mistake, we would never even have learned how to walk as toddlers. We have to find some way of overcoming the wall of fear which stops us taking risk, learning new things and striving for success.

In practice, this means you have to learn how to control your internal chatter. At moments of truth, the chatter becomes deafening as the angels of hope compete with the demons of fear for your attention. The angels of hope will assure you that you can succeed and that success will be worthwhile. The demons of fear will paint a picture of failure leading to disaster for you professionally and personally. It is a debate that the demons of fear can easily win: we are all attuned to be loss-averse.

Your challenge is to manage your demons of fear. The surprising solution is to listen to your demons closely and then challenge them. Trying to shut the demons down or ignore them simply will not work. If you ignore your demons, they will just try harder and harder to gain your attention: they will become that nagging doubt that will not go away. Your demons will slowly undermine your confidence and make failure more likely. They become a self-fulfilling prophecy.

Far from ignoring the demons of fear, encourage them:

1. Ask your demons what is the worst thing that can happen.
2. Ask whether you can survive the worst case.
3. Ask what the best case can be.
4. Ask what you need to do to move from worst to best case.

Exercise 9: listen to your internal chatter[40]

When you next face a difficult situation or choice, follow the four steps below. Do not try to run away from your demons: you can only tame them by listening to them constructively.

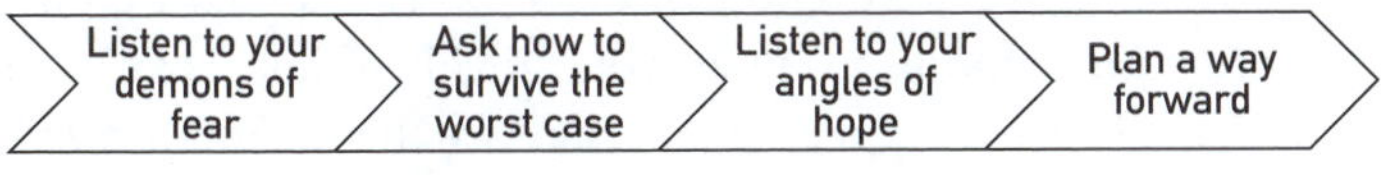

Figure 2.1 Demons and angels

Fear of failure

I decided to start a bank. This requires at least $1 billion of capital. I checked my bank account and found that I was more than $1 billion short of the required funding.

The chances of failure were high. All the experts took great delight in pointing out the many flaws in my idea: where would I find $1 billion (short of robbing a bank to start a bank), how would I build all the technology, how would I overcome resistance of regulators to a new bank, where would I find the team and how would I stop the big competitors crushing the idea?

The fear of failure came in three flavours. Financial failure could be bad: in the worst case I could lose everything, including my house. Professional failure would make financial failure worse: would I be able to get another job and rebuild my career after such a spectacular failure? Finally, there was the fear of personal failure: I would become a laughing stock among my peers, friends and family for taking on such an absurd challenge.

Instead of running away from these fears, I confronted them. I realised I could manage the financial risk. I had confidence in my

> professional skills to rebuild a career if necessary and being mocked socially was the least of my worries. Only after I had faced my fears could I conquer them and find the courage to leave my job and pursue the new bank. The result was that I could commit to the new venture 100%, which was essential to success.

If you look at the worst case and know you can survive, then making the brave decision becomes much easier.

Once your demons know they have been heard and recognised, they calm down. They accept that the risk has been acknowledged and dealt with: they do not need to start shouting louder and louder. If you try to ignore your demons, they will go berserk. Once your demons go quiet, your angels of hope have a chance of being heard. Listen to them: they are the future that you want to create. Once you have listened to both angels and demons, you can start to work out how to move away from the worst case and achieve the best case. You will be able to look at the situation rationally and objectively, not through the foggy lens of fear and hope.

Learning to manage your demons and angels is vital for resilience and sustaining high performance. If you let your demons take over, you will never learn, grow and fulfil your potential. When you start to hear your demons of fear start to chatter, do not ignore them: listen to them because they are trying to help you. Make the simple four-step approach in Figure 2.1 a standard habit, and you will find that your angels and demons can have a smart conversation that will lead you to the right way forward.

Summary

Negative emotions, like pain, serve a very useful purpose. They tell us that something is wrong and that we need to do something about it. Like pain, negative emotions are also dangerous if they are ignored. The negative emotions can become a state of mind that saps your energy, reduces motivation, makes risk-taking impossible, inhibits learning and leads to low performance. This means you have to learn to manage negative emotions.

The first surprise to many people is that you have a choice about how you feel. If you feel happy or miserable that is largely your choice. There are clearly extremes, such as winning the lottery or going to prison which will affect your immediate wellbeing. But apart from these extremes, there is no need to be a victim where your emotions are dictated to you by other people's conduct.

"You have a choice about how you feel."

Awareness is your vital gateway to choice and control. You can only control your feelings if you are aware of them and if you are aware that you have a choice about how you feel. Once you know you have a choice, then you can exercise control using the simple how-why-what process:

- How do I feel?
- Why do I feel that way?
- What do I want to do about it?

Fear is a particularly difficult feeling to manage, because it has always been vital to our survival. Fear of failure is also learned through school and work. If fear stops you taking risks, learning new skills or taking on challenging people and situations, you can never succeed. Fear stops you failing, but it also stops you succeeding.

"Negative emotions, like pain, serve a very useful purpose."

Courage to deal with fear can be learned in two ways. The firemen and Marines way is by gentling stretching yourself: slowly make the unfamiliar feel familiar and the risky seem routine. The second way is to manage your internal chatter between the demons of fear and angels of hope. Since you cannot ignore the demons of fear, confront them directly. Once the demons have been heard, they will settle down and you can listen to the angels of hope.

Sustaining long-term success depends on managing your emotions and managing your hopes and fears.

Chapter 3

Be kind to yourself: the power of FAST thinking

This chapter is about building resilience in real time. It will show you how you can capture unproductive thought habits and make them more helpful in the moment. You will discover two core techniques:

- How you can choose to react to adversity positively by challenging unhelpful beliefs.
- How you can stop the five classic mind traps from sinking you.

This chapter is all about managing your internal dialogue. We can often be our own harshest critics. By controlling your internal chatter you can learn to be kind to yourself and help yourself react better and perform better. It will show you how you can develop Fast, Accurate and Self-enhancing Thinking: think FAST in real time.

Why it matters

It was not just a traffic jam: it was gridlock. I was rapidly going nowhere. As I gazed out of the windscreen I started to people watch. Two lanes to my left, a middle-aged man had succumbed to the red mist. He was gesticulating wildly at the vehicles around him. He would occasionally pump his car horn to vent his anger, in the vain hope that sounding his horn would make the traffic vanish.

Immediately to my right, a business woman had recreated her office in the back of a cab: she had papers all around her, a laptop on her lap and she cradled a phone on her shoulder as she talked and typed at the same time. She was oblivious to the rest of the world. This meant she probably missed the performance in front of her as a young couple decided to make the most of their time together and they were lost in each other's arms. Other drivers gazed nowhere, listened to the radio or fidgeted. But none of us was going anywhere.

Gridlock is an equal opportunity irritation: it treats everyone just the same, regardless of who you are. But everyone was reacting differently. At that moment, I realised that you can choose how you react to adversity. Gridlock can be annoying, especially if you are running late for a vital meeting or a flight. But there is no law that says you have to be annoyed: being annoyed is a personal choice. You can choose how you react: you can sound your horn, you can whisper sweet nothings to your lover, you can chill out and listen to music, you can set up your office or you can people watch.

This was my eureka moment: you can choose how you feel. You do not need to have your feelings imposed on you by events or by other people. This was liberation: I no longer needed to be a victim of the world. I could choose for myself.

"Gridlock is an equal opportunity irritation."

But then the questions started to flood in:

- Why do some people get angry and others stay calm in exactly the same situation?
- How can you ensure you make the right choice in the heat of the moment?
- How do your choices affect your life outcomes?

"You can choose how you feel."

Over the coming months and years, I slowly put the pieces together. I was less interested in the theory, and more interested in the practice. I was fed up with being pessimistic and cynical and I was fed up with being fed up. I wanted to make better choices for myself.

"I was fed up with being fed up."

The first step was the traffic jam discovery. The Newtonian world of physics does not apply to how we think: one action does not lead to the same reaction for everyone. One action leads to many different reactions. Somewhere there was a missing piece. That missing piece turns out to be our beliefs about ourselves and our world.

In the Newtonian world, an apple always falls downwards off a tree. You would be very surprised if you walked into an orchard and saw apples falling upwards, or sideways. Being attacked by an apple would make an interesting crime report or insurance claim. If we are like apples and we all react the same way to an event, we become victims of fate, just like the apples. Events clearly can shape our mood. If your boss shouts at you, that is rarely a moment to laugh and rejoice. Weddings are normally joyous and funerals mournful.

But even these extreme events can defy the stereotype: some funerals turn into celebrations of the deceased's life and a chance for friends and family to reconnect. Some weddings degenerate into fights as the two families fall out after too much alcohol. There is no action which leads to an inevitable human reaction.

In the new world, the radical difference is the mediating effect of our beliefs. It is not just the event that determines how we feel and how we act. Our beliefs shape our reactions.

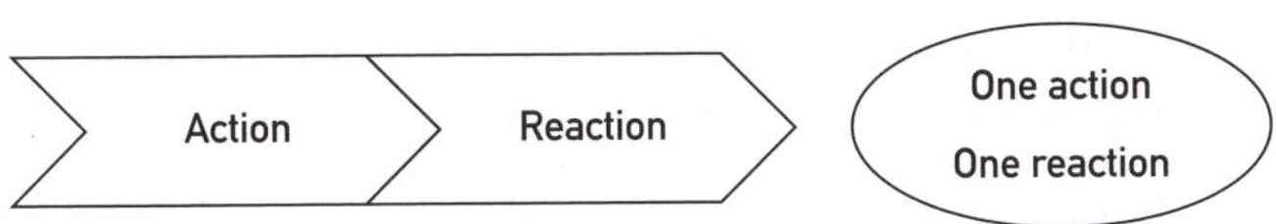

Figure 3.1 The Newtonian world

Figure 3.2 New world

"Our beliefs shape our reactions."

The challenge is that many of our beliefs are so deep that they are hidden from ourselves. Our beliefs are like our operating system. Few of us care to dive into the operating system of our computer to try and understand it and change it. Few of us care to dive into the operating system of our brain and examine the core beliefs that determine how we feel and how we act.

"Our beliefs are so deep that they are hidden from ourselves."

If it is hard to explore the operating system of our beliefs, it is even harder to change them. Our beliefs make us who we are. Our beliefs have enabled us to get to where we are in life, for better or for worse. In practice, this means that our beliefs have worked at least in some conditions and some circumstances. But even the most successful people find that their beliefs can trip them up at just the wrong moment. This means that you do not need to change your beliefs: you need to understand them and recognise when they are going to help you and when they are going to hinder you.

Most of the time, you will be thinking and acting intuitively, because that is the most practical way to navigate the world. This is what Nobel Prize Laureate called thinking fast. [41] But he showed that you also need to be able to think slow, to challenge yourself when it matters.

This chapter will show how you can identify and manage your beliefs in context.

Cultivate the habit: the FAST approach

As a child, I learned a game where you have to avoid stepping on the cracks between paving stones or a bear or a snake would come out of the crack and eat you. So I learned to hop from one paving stone to the next. I still do, when I am bored. It has proven to be a good strategy because I have avoided being eaten by a snake or a bear, so far. But in practice, if we always had to be looking out for bears and snakes hiding in every corner, we would never go anywhere. If we had to do a full engineering study of every bridge we wanted to cross to make sure it was safe, we would be stuck.

We have to make simplifying assumptions about how the world works. We assume that cracks between paving stones are safe, bridges are safe, we will not get mugged while doing the grocery shopping, that the food we buy will not make us ill, and that the plane we fly in will not fall out of the sky. When these assumptions prove false, there is immediate media outrage.

These assumptions extend to how we interact with other people. But everyone has different assumptions about what works and what does not work. Some people think you can trust colleagues while others disagree. Some people think it is good to take risk, others prefer safety first. Like the assumption that bridges are safe, these assumptions are so deep that we do not even realise that we are making them. This makes your assumptions both very useful and very dangerous.

> “Your assumptions cannot always be correct in every context.”

Your assumptions are useful because they make navigating day-to-day life easy: you do not have to think deeply about every action you take. But they are also very dangerous because your assumptions cannot always be correct in every context. The assumption of trusting people can get you into trouble. The assumption of not taking risks means you may miss endless opportunities.

These assumptions are your belief system, your operating system that enables you to function from day to day. They are the beliefs that determine how you react to events, so it is worth understanding your beliefs and how they help or hinder you.

Ideally, you will have beliefs that represent Flexible, Accurate and Self-enhancing Thinking, or FAST thinking. It has to be fast, because you need to be able to react in real time. Here is what FAST stands for:

- **Flexible:** Different events require different reactions. For instance, believing that you should not quit is clearly helpful if it means you persevere with difficult challenges. It could be fatal if it means you fail to turn back from near the summit of Everest with a storm approaching. You can recognise inflexible thinking when your internal chatter starts to use absolute words like 'must, never, no one, always, everyone, ought'. When you hear these words in your mind, challenge them. Is it really true that you should never quit, even if it means you die and do not reach your goal of climbing your Everest? Is it really true that you can never trust anyone? Inflexible thinking cannot be accurate 100% of the time. You need flexibility in your thinking to make it accurate and helpful in your situation.
- **Accurate:** It is easy to react emotionally and negatively to events. Then we use evidence like a drunk uses a lamp post: for support, not illumination. We use evidence to confirm our feelings. Accurate thinking avoids all the big mind traps and lets us assess the evidence accurately. This illuminates your position and lets you make better and well-informed choices about how to react.

"We use evidence like a drunk uses a lamp post: for support, not illumination."

- **Self-enhancing:** Some beliefs are helpful, while others are less helpful. We have already seen that optimistic thinking will help you live longer and function better than pessimistic thinking. Having a sense of agency is better than believing that you are a victim of fate, while having a sense of self-worth is better than not having a sense of self-worth. Often, we can be our own worst critics. Our internal chatter can be cruel to us. Self-enhancing chatter is like having your best friend talk to you.

- **Thinking:** The real challenge with our beliefs is that we are unaware of them: they let us react instinctively and reflexively to events. This works most of the time and helps us. But, occasionally, your instincts will get you into trouble and you find yourself reacting in unhelpful ways. In the heat of the moment, it is often impossible to change course. But, after the event, it is worth reflecting on why you reacted as you did. If you are not aware of your beliefs, you cannot manage them. You have to discover your iceberg beliefs: you can find out how to do this later in this chapter.

"We can be our own worst critics."

Exercise 10: challenge your thinking at work

This is an exercise that all good leader writers do when writing an opinion piece. First, they will write the piece from the opposite side of their perspective. Only when they fully understand their opponent's view, can they demolish it. You can apply the same sort of exercise at work.

1. Review a current or recent dispute with a colleague or friend. You can find plenty of reasons why you are right. Now construct the argument from the other side: how will they portray events? You can be sure that their narrative shows that they are in the right. Once you understand how they see the world, you have a chance of showing some empathy and understanding, and you can find a way forward. Or you can decide to deal even more forcibly with them.
2. If you are preparing a major pitch for your idea, look at it from the perspective of the people you are pitching to. What do they really want? What do they like and dislike? What are their alternatives? What objections might they have? Once you see the

world through their eyes, you are more likely to persuade them and you are less likely to be tripped up by unexpected questions and problems. This perspective stops you falling in love with your idea and ignoring the needs and reality of the decision-makers.

Looking at alternative perspectives is highly effective. It makes you a much more disciplined and creative thinker and a much more effective persuader at work.

Portraits of resilience: FAST thinking

Cathy O'Dowd, the first woman to climb Everest

"Climbing is always about choices," says Cathy, the first woman to climb Everest from both the north and south sides. And, sometimes, those choices are about life and death because "climbing always has two goals: to get to the summit, and to get down safely again".

Making clear choices under pressure is always hard. Making life and death choices when you are near the summit of Everest and you are cold, exhausted and short of oxygen is much harder. She faced a real life and death choice when she came across a dying climber near the summit. Do you stop and help, turn back or go on? After one hour of trying to help the dying climber, Cathy turned back. In her words: "If you get summit fever and then collapse at the top, you give your team a problem. They have to carry you down. Unlike a marathon, you cannot stop and call a taxi."

The same clarity helped her on an unclimbed route up Nanga Parbat (the world's ninth highest mountain). They were out of food, faced a two-day exit down an unknown route and had sherpas who knew Everest: wrong mountain. Two team members pressed ahead, ready to risk everything to reach the top. She turned back because she was clear about her choices and her goals: "I am in it for a lifetime of climbing. I want to be climbing at the age of 80. Always know what you want."

Sometimes, success must be postponed. We always have choices, even if they are uncomfortable choices.

Like many resilient people, she knows her resilience is contextual: "I am more resilient to risk in mountains because I have put the hours in and know my strengths and weaknesses." Her resilience draws on experience and learning (Chapter 9), reaching out and working with experienced mountaineers (Chapter 5), a high degree of goal focus (Chapter 8) and self-efficacy (Chapter 4).

"We always have choices, even if they are uncomfortable choices."

The table below illustrates the differences between flexible and inflexible thinking, and between self-enhancing and self-defeating beliefs.

	Self-defeating	**Self-enhancing**
Flexible	*Pessimism* I prefer not to trust people The world is a risky place I dislike asking for help	*Optimism and growth* I prefer to trust and respect people I like to learn and grow It is worth making an effort
Inflexible	*Victim mindset* Never trust anyone No one likes me I am a victim of cruel fate	*Narcissm, over achievement* I must win/succeed/be perfect I must be liked by everyone I must be in charge

In practice, your beliefs are your beliefs. Changing your beliefs is the same as changing who you are. Maybe that is what you either want or need to do, in which case you may well be able to help make a psychotherapist rich. It takes time, hard work and a lot of support to change your beliefs.

You have a simpler option, which lets you remain as you are, does not require a long course of psychotherapy and is fast. It is about helping yourself become more flexible and adaptable to different situations. It is a wonderful way to use adversity. Every time you find yourself over-reacting to a small event, the chances are that you have just encountered one of your iceberg beliefs. These are your deep beliefs, which help you most of the time but sometimes hole you beneath the water line.

"Changing your beliefs is the same as changing who you are."

Use each iceberg event to reveal more about your iceberg beliefs. These events are often the only way you find out what your iceberg beliefs are, so they are very valuable to you. If you are annoyed or upset by an event, use the event to your advantage: identify your beliefs that caused you to be upset. You can then modify them if you think they need modification. You do not need to abandon your beliefs: you need to identify them and identify the circumstances where they may or may not work for you.

For instance, I have an iceberg belief that respect is earned not given. What's not to like about that? It means that I have to work hard to prove myself the whole time. When I chair various boards, I never assume that I deserve respect: respect comes from doing a good job, not from your title. But even this apparently innocent belief has a dark side. It means that I have a complete lack of respect for authority or arbitrary rules. Just because someone is in power does not mean they have to be respected if they act stupidly.

That is a recipe for getting into trouble repeatedly, with both important people and with petty officials who enforce dumb rules. It was a catastrophic belief to have at school. The violent reaction of teachers to my lack of respect for some of them simply reinforced my belief that respect should be earned, not given. That is the nature of beliefs: we interpret events in such a way that they are constantly reinforced. This is called confirmation bias and it creates a validation loop that is hard to escape.

So I have identified my iceberg belief and I am happy to live with it. But now I know that there are circumstances where it is not a helpful belief. Slowly, I have learned to modify my belief. So now I recognise that although respect should be earned and power should be obeyed (even if not respected), that then becomes consistent with other personal beliefs such as that conflict is undesirable.

The key is to understand where your beliefs help or hinder you. This is a process of discovery. If you make it a process of purposeful discovery, you can introduce flexibility into your thinking so that you react appropriately in different contexts. Examples of how beliefs help and hinder in different contexts are in the table below.

By definition, most of your iceberg beliefs exist beneath the surface and are hard to find. This section gives you two exercises to help you find and challenge your iceberg beliefs.

Exercise 11: identify your iceberg beliefs

Below is a table with some of the more common iceberg beliefs. Review the table and see if you have any of the beliefs. All of them have positive consequences which will help you most of the time. They also have negative consequences which can trip you up occasionally. If you have none of these beliefs, you can use the table below as a prompt to think about what iceberg beliefs you do have, and then think about how they help you most of the time and how they might hinder you sometimes.

This exercise is fundamentally about building awareness. Once you are aware that you may have some iceberg beliefs, you can start to manage them. If you are not aware of them, you become a prisoner of their consequences.

Belief	Positive consequence	Negative consequence
Failure is a sign of weakness	Determined to achieve	Avoid taking risky or stretching roles
I must be liked	Collegial and kind	Inability to start difficult conversations (about performance, expectations, etc.)

Belief	Positive consequence	Negative consequence
Conflict is undesirable	Cooperative and amenable	Failure to stand up to bullies and conflict, easy pushover
Respect is earned not given	Work, achievement focus	Lack of respect for authority and arbitrary rules lead to trouble
My time is valuable	Work hard	Easily irritated by queues and other people
Women should be kind and supportive	Helpful team player	Failure to stand up for own interests
A real man never shows emotion	Strong task focus	Unresolved anguish, low emotional intelligence in dealing with colleagues
A real man never quits	Perseverance in the face of adversity	Persist where it is dangerous (on a mountain) or dysfunctional (in a bad job)
Anyone who disagrees with my faith or politics is evil	Commitment to a cause	Lapse into violence and extremism
Follow your passion	Potential to achieve excellence	What effect will this have on your family?
Integrity is everything	Strong role model	Intolerance of others

Belief	Positive consequence	Negative consequence
Colleagues are in it for themselves and cannot be trusted	Politically astute	Working alone, failure to build networks of support
I must be respected	Strive to do the right thing	Quick to take offence
Hard work leads to success	Hard work	Reluctance to deal with politics of work
My wedding or birthday should be perfect	Focus on creating a magical day	Disappointment and tears with any minor setback or blemish

Exercise 12: challenge your iceberg beliefs

Often it is not possible to identify iceberg beliefs until you hit the iceberg. These are the moments in life when things go wrong for you. Although painful, these moments are highly valuable. They are a great opportunity to spot your iceberg belief and then challenge it so that you can deal with it more productively in future.

You can challenge your iceberg beliefs in a structured way. Here is a three-step approach for managing your iceberg beliefs productively. It is an exercise worth doing with someone else who can ask you the questions in step two. The act of talking through your answers normally reveals a clarity that is not there when the windmills of your mind are spinning round and round.

1. **Stop:** Be aware of your reactions. Awareness is the gateway to choice and control. It is too easy to dismiss an adverse event as

bad luck or to blame it on another person. But if you reacted in an unhelpful way, you were making choices that caused that to happen. That is a good moment to stop yourself, but not to blame yourself. Simply note that you had an unhelpful reaction to a difficult situation.

2. **Reflect:** Identify the iceberg belief that caused you to react that way. Ask yourself some simple 'what' questions, in any order:
   - What was the worst part of that for me?
   - What does that mean to me?
   - What was the most upsetting part of that for me?
   - Assuming all that is true, what makes that so upsetting to me now?

   These questions will let you be open and honest with yourself. Asking yourself why it all went wrong just leads to post-rationalisation and defensiveness, even in your own internal chatter. Asking the what questions allows you to blow off steam, while revealing the iceberg thought at the same time.
3. **Refine:** Identify how you can adapt your belief to make it more flexible and suit different situations better. You should not attack your belief. It is better to understand your belief than to judge it. You can do this by asking three questions, in order:
   - Where has that belief helped you in the past? Reinforce to yourself that your beliefs have value, at least in some circumstances. Be specific about how it has helped you.
   - How did it not help you on this occasion?
   - How could you adapt the belief to make it more helpful to you in similar situations in future?

In workshops, the hardest and most productive step is step two. It is the moment where clarity comes out and step three becomes easy. In real life, the hardest step is step 1: take time to stop and to catch yourself thinking in a way that is unhelpful. Simply stopping and challenging yourself is very powerful.

Iceberg beliefs and developing flexible thinking

Situation: My boss cancelled my big presentation to the board which I have been working on for weeks. She says that she will take up my proposal directly with the CEO.

Step 1: Stop

Stop getting angry about your boss, who may have been helping you get your proposal accepted by going through the back door (a chat with the CEO) than by going through the front door (a presentation to the board).

Step 2: Reflect

What does that mean to you? It means that my proposal is delayed at best, and it means that my work will not be seen by the board, so that means my promotion hopes are dead. I cannot trust my boss any more and I am no longer on speaking terms with her.

What was most upsetting about that to you? It shows that she does not trust me at all. If you cannot trust your boss, it's time to get another boss.

What was the worst part of that for you? I thought I could rely on my boss. But I can't. It means there is no one I can rely on.

Reflection quickly revealed a core belief: "I should be able to trust or rely on my boss." This caused chaos when, for potentially very good reasons, the boss decided to manage a decision differently from the way that had been agreed previously.

Step 3: Refine

Where has that belief helped you in the past? It has been really helpful in getting me interesting work. I have learned huge amounts and it has led to promotion.

How did that belief not help you on this occasion? It meant that I let myself become dependent on one person to promote me and protect all my interests.

How could you adapt the belief in future? I still want to keep the belief, but, in future, I will build my network of support so that I do not have to rely completely on one person's good will.

In this case, the belief remains the same (trust the boss) but the behaviour becomes more flexible and productive. Instead of blind trust in one person, and gambling everything on that relationship, you might decide to build a broader base of support across the organisation. This will give you more options and more information about how to play different situations.

Laid out as text, this looks like a long process. In practice, it can take a few moments or minutes as you quietly reflect on what happened over a cup of coffee.

Cultivate the habit: managing the big five mind traps and developing your explanatory style

We all tell ourselves stories about why things happen. We want to find reasons for everything. Even if we cannot find a rational reason, we still want to find a story to explain the inexplicable. In similar fashion, superstition, magic and religion have provided answers for questions that we cannot answer through reason. As humans, we always seek a reason for what happens. The way we explain things to ourselves matters for our resilience. FAST thinking is a way of helping us understand and explain our reactions to adversity more productively.

Sometimes, our thinking is helpful and, sometimes, it is not. There are five classic mindset traps that we all fall into from time to time. These traps are all ways of explaining adversity to ourselves, and they are all deeply unhelpful. It is worth noting these mind traps. If you find yourself using them, wave the red flag mentally. These explanatory methods will not help you. The five mind traps are:

- catastrophising
- helplessness
- mind-reading
- personalising
- externalising.

Exercise 13: identify your mind traps

This exercise is about raising awareness. It is a simple way of inoculating yourself against the most common and dangerous traps everyone falls into from time to time. Review and remember these five mind traps. Recall when you (or someone near to you) fell into this mind trap. What were the consequences? There are some suggestions on how you can deal with each mind trap. This is a cheat sheet to help you in adversity.

Catastrophising

This mind trap is easy to spot. You are likely to be catastrophising when your internal chatter starts to use permanent and pervasive words such as 'always, never, no one, everyone, nothing and everything'. For instance, this is a catastrophic way of responding to a setback: "No one ever helps me. It is impossible to get anything done. Nothing ever works properly here."

From catastrophising to helplessness is a very small step. If you really do believe that no one ever helps and that it is impossible to make things happen, then you may as well give up right away. Resilience flies out of the window when catastrophising walks in through the door.

When you catastrophise, your mind will search for all the evidence that you are right. It will be seeking confirmation of the beliefs such as my boss can never be trusted and my colleagues never help. When you hear catastrophic language like that, challenge it. Instead of searching for confirming evidence, search for evidence that contradicts your belief. You will quickly find there is an alternative perspective.

If you think that your colleagues never help you, you can find plenty of evidence to confirm your belief. Instead, challenge your belief and find the occasions where they have helped you. You will quickly find evidence that colleagues will help you under the right circumstances. So, then you can think about creating the conditions where colleagues will help you. You will have turned catastrophic thinking into constructive thinking.

Helplessness

This is where you believe that nothing can be done to change your situation: you are simply a victim of a cruel world. This belief can creep up on you. After a hundred job applications and no interviews, it is easy to start to believe that nothing will work (catastrophising), so you may as well give up (helplessness).

This 'learned helplessness' was first observed by the godfather of positive psychology, Professor Martin Seligman.[42] In the days when it was fine to give dogs electric shocks, he gave shocks to three groups of dogs. The first set of dogs had a control which they could press to stop the shocks. The second group had the shocks but no control. The third group had neither the shocks nor the control button. He then moved the dogs to shock treatment phase two: the dogs were given shocks in a small pen with a low wall which they could easily jump over. The dogs in group one (which previously had the control button) and in group three (which previously had no shocks) easily jumped over the low wall to escape the shocks. The dogs in group two (which previously had the shocks and no way of controlling them) had learned that they could not control electric shocks. Although they could easily escape, they just lay there and whimpered. They had learned to be helpless.

At work, helplessness comes about when you rely too much on your boss, the system or colleagues to do things for you. It is a seductive trap to fall into: as long as your boss is covering for you, life is good. When the boss moves on or lets you down, it comes as a big shock. You will not have acquired the routines and networks to succeed. As we shall see in the next chapter, learned helplessness outside work can kill you.

"Helplessness comes about when you rely too much on your boss."

Mind-reading

Mind-reading is a good way to destroy relationships. It will also help you misinterpret events and it will let you leap to judgements about people and colleagues in a way that encourages conflict and prevents any resolution. It is a vicious and nasty mind trap because it not only damages you, it damages your colleagues, friends and family as well.

This mind trap is evident if you catch yourself saying things like: "You don't really mean that, you're not really sorry, you are just saying that to please me, you don't really want to go or you're just pretending ..." This language boxes the other person into a corner. Anything they say will simply confirm the judgement you have already made, and the result is resentment and argument. It is very rare to have a positive outcome to a mind-reading conversation.

> **"Mind-reading is a good way to destroy relationships."**

If you find yourself about to come up with some mind-reading statements, stop yourself. Instead of making statements, ask open questions such as:

- Why do you say that?
- What do you mean by that?
- How does that work?

Asking questions helps you in two ways. First, it buys you time. You give yourself the chance to come up with a more considered reaction to your partner. Second, you may discover something useful about what your partner really intended. With better information you can find a better response.

Externalising

We all externalise from time to time: we blame the world on our misfortune, not ourselves. This is natural. We are all heroes of our own life story, and it does not fit the heroic narrative to say that we've messed up. Externalising too much means you lose agency: you will start to believe that you are a victim of fate (or of other people) beyond your control. By externalising the blame for your setbacks, you never learn from them. Externalising is another road that leads to helplessness.

If you externalise your problems and keep on blaming your colleagues or team members, you will quickly lose trust in them. You will then find it harder to work with your peers or to delegate to your team. You become an island, and that is not the path to success in an organisation. All organisations are based on collaboration, they are not based on working by yourself. In extreme cases, externalising means that you end up arguing and fighting with colleagues as you seek to blame them for any setback.

"We are all heroes of our own life story."

Personalising

Personalising is the opposite of externalising. This is where you blame yourself for everything, all the time. It is accountability taken to an extreme. It quickly leads to a valley of death experience where you start to think that you can never achieve anything. Personalising is the gateway to catastrophising.

"Personalising is the gateway to catastrophising."

When you find yourself falling into these mind traps, challenge them because they are not helping you. You need to be able to challenge these mind traps positively and productively. You can do this by playing a game, which is the game used as tie breakers in competitions where you have to complete a sentence in no more than 12 words saying why you think Sudso (or some other miracle product) is wonderful.

Here are three tie-breaker sentences for you to complete. By completing them, you will challenge your thinking and find a more productive explanation of events:

That's not completely true because ...

Mind trap explanations are rarely true, even if they contain a grain of truth. This is where confirmation bias comes from. If you are thinking that everyone is against me and nothing is working, you will be able to find evidence that someone is against you and some things are not working. That could allow you to confirm your view that everyone is against you and nothing is working.

By completing "That is not completely true because ..." you force yourself to find the evidence that shows that not everyone is against you and maybe some things can work. You quickly move from a position of helplessness to a position where you have options and you can take back control.

A more optimistic way of seeing this is ...

Again, let's assume you have started by thinking that everyone is against me and nothing works. A more optimistic way of seeing this might be:

- I have learned many valuable lessons here which will help me avoid pain and disappointment in future.
- Setbacks like this will make success in the future all the sweeter.
- Despite going through this bad patch, I have survived. And I know from my past I can achieve great things, so I am confident I can achieve great things in the future.
- This has been a huge test of my resilience, which will make me stronger in the future.

I can improve things by ...

This question is worth asking last. If your starting point is that everyone is against me and nothing works, then you will not believe you can improve things, unless you have asked yourself the first two questions. When you ask this question, you will be ready to drive to action. Curiously, the worse the situation becomes, the simpler your choices become, because you may only have one possible course of action, which may be to speak to your boss, best friend or spouse.

When you ask this question, do not ruminate over each idea. You will persuade yourself that each idea is no good if you are in a bad mood. Generate as many ideas as you can without judging them. By the time you have 10 or 12 ideas in front of you, at least you will realise that you have choices, even if the choices are not all comfortable. Once you have choices, you start to regain control: you can choose what you do instead of responding to cruel fate.

Exercise 14: cope with your mind traps

When you find yourself falling into any of the classic mind traps, challenge your thinking by attempting to complete the following three sentences:

1. That is not completely true because ...
2. A more optimistic way of seeing this is ...
3. I can improve things by ...

Completing these sentences will help you see your reality in a more positive, constructive and actionable light.

Summary

The big lesson is that how you react and feel about events is your choice. If you are angry, happy, sad, bored or frustrated, those are choices you make. Choice means you are in control, you are not a victim of fate. Your choices are driven by your beliefs, which may be so deep that they are hidden from view: they are iceberg beliefs.

Your beliefs are vital simplifying assumptions about how you think the world works or should work. They probably work for you most of the time, but will occasionally fail you. That is when you need to look for your icebergs in three steps:

1. Stop. Be aware of your reaction and how it helped or hindered you.
2. Reflect. Identify the belief that led to your reaction by asking what questions: What does that mean to me and what was the worst part of that?
3. Refine. Identify how you can adapt your belief to make it more flexible and suit different situations better. Don't try to attack your beliefs, because that is an attack on yourself. Simplify and

modify your beliefs for different contexts. Be flexible. Avoid the most common mind traps:

- Catastrophising: Nothing, no one, never, always, everyone.
- Helplessness: Becoming the victim of cruel fate, believing nothing is possible.
- Mind-reading: You don't really mean that, you're not really sorry.
- Personalising: Everything in the world is my fault.
- Externalising: Everyone else is at fault, except me.

You can challenge these mind traps by playing the competition tie breaker game. Complete in a few words any of the following three sentences:

- That is not completely true because ...
- A more optimistic way of seeing this is ...
- I can improve things by ...

These mind tools are designed to help you have FAST thinking:

- Flexible: Have beliefs that adapt to each situation appropriately.
- Accurate: Assess situations accurately and avoid common mind traps.
- Self-enhancing: As opposed to negative and destructive.
- Thinking: Be aware of your thinking and choose actively how you react.

FAST thinking enables you to build your resilience in real time.

Chapter

Control your destiny: the power of self-belief

We live in a world where we have more freedom but more responsibility than ever before. The old certainties have been cast away and instead we live with ambiguity, opportunity and uncertainty. In this new world, you have to take control of your destiny rather than be controlled by events. Self-efficacy enables you to achieve your goals better, whether they are personal goals, such as health, fitness and diet, or career goals.

This chapter introduces two core concepts that will allow you to take control: self-efficacy and locus of control. It will then give you four core exercises to help you achieve self-efficacy:

1. Stritstery.
2. Deal with setbacks: watch the movie (not the snapshot).
3. Reach out.
4. Build your influence

Why self-efficacy matters at work and in life

Charles Stanley was a Texas cowboy who transformed himself into the Rattlesnake King.[43] In the 1870s, he took up with some Hopi Indians, from whom he claimed to have learned the secret healing powers of rattlesnake oil. Charles Stanley had found his destiny: he was no longer a cowboy, he became the original snake oil salesman. He put on shows where he pulled a live snake out of a bag, slit it open and then plunged it into boiling water. He then skimmed the fat off the top and used it to create, on the spot, his snake oil linament, which was reputed to cure more or less everything that could afflict you on the frontier.

Demand for the snake oil far outstripped the supply of snakes. In 1917, Federal Investigators[44] found that his snake oil contained precisely no snake: it was a potent mix of beef fat, red pepper and turpentine. He was fined a grand total of $20, but had already made his fortune from 17 factories which churned out his snake-free snake oil.

So what would you do if you were offered a miracle drug today that would help you achieve all your lifestyle goals, such as getting down to your ideal weight, quitting smoking, controlling your drinking, and help you take on and achieve challenging tasks at work? You might conclude you were buying more snake oil from the modern-day equivalent of the Rattlesnake King.

The surprise is that there is something that can help you achieve all these difficult goals, and it does not involve killing and boiling snakes. It is not even a drug. The miracle cure is all in your mind, and it is a combination of two closely related ideas:

- **Self-efficacy:**[45] This is the belief that you can accomplish your goals, in the face of both unexpected and adverse events.
- **Locus of control:**[46] This is the belief that you are in control of your destiny and that you are not the victim of fate.

"The miracle cure is all in your mind."

If you already score well on these beliefs, you will think that they are obvious. On a good day, we probably all feel that we are masters of our fate and that we can achieve our goals. But resilience is not about how you feel when you are living in easy street: it is about how you manage when times are tough. This chapter will show you how these beliefs will not only help you perform better at work, but they will even help you live longer. Like optimism, these are very powerful beliefs to have. Also like optimism, these are habits of mind that you can nurture with some simple exercises.

Self-efficacy and locus of control in the workplace

In practice, the need for strong self-efficacy and locus of control is increasing in the workplace. The world of work is changing. In the past, the role of middle management was to transmit orders down the hierarchy, and to filter information back up. That is no longer the case. Now you really have to manage: make decisions, have difficult conversations, persuade, motivate, deal with crises, solve problems and manage a world that is becoming more volatile, uncertain, complex and ambiguous (VUCA).[47] This is a world where you have to believe that:

- you can accomplish your goals in the face of adverse and unexpected events (self-efficacy)
- you are in control of events, and that you are not a mere cipher transmitting orders and information up and down the hierarchy (locus of control).

The power of self-efficacy and locus of control was shown in extreme form by Steve Jobs, the legendary co-founder of Apple. He famously had a 'reality distortion field':[48] he would bend the world to his will through a mixture of charm, brilliance and bullying. Andy Mackenzie recalls starting work for Apple in 1981, and finding that he was responsible for shipping the software for the new Mac computer in ten months' time. No one had even started the work. Andy turned to his boss Bud Tribble, and told him the schedule was not just impossible, but crazy as well. Bud then described Steve's reality distortion field which simply did not recognise words like schedule or impossible. Somehow, the Mac shipped on time.

Steve Jobs' reality distortion field was not confined to dealing with his team. His MacWorld events became cult events in which Apple enthusiasts would come to hear Steve declare that Apple's latest products were 'insanely great'. He created a sense of enthusiasm and commitment to the brand which no other software or hardware group has come close to emulating.

Plenty of other entrepreneurs and leaders have been attributed with a reality distortion field, for better or worse, including Bill

Clinton, Donald Trump and Elon Musk.[49] All of them, in their own ways, believe that they can bend the world to their will.

If a reality distortion field is an extreme form of locus of control, there is a milder version for the other 99.99% of us who are mere mortals. This version was summed up in the best book you never need to buy, which is called *Control Your Destiny or Someone Else Will*.[50] The book describes how long-serving GE boss Jack Welch built the firm. But the real value of the book is the title itself. Once you have read the title, you have the one message you should take home with you: everything else is detail.

The challenge is that the nature of control is changing. In the past, control was about power and authority. The higher you climbed the organisational ladder, the more power and the more control you had. This is only partially true today. You still have more power at the top than at the bottom of the firm. But wherever you are, you cannot rely on formal authority alone. Increasingly, if you want to make things happen, you have to rely on the arts of influence and persuasion:[51] building the right networks of support, creating trusted alliances, forging common agendas, resolving conflicts and stepping up at moments of crisis and uncertainty.

"If you want to make things happen you have to rely on the arts of influence and persuasion."

Locus of control is not about your position and power, it is about how you think and act. Controlling, or at least influencing, your destiny means different things at different times:

- Good times: Make sure you get the right assignments, learning, bonus and promotion opportunities.
- Tough times: Deal with crises, setbacks and conflicts which means stepping up, not back.
- Normal times: Show that you are on top of your brief, your projects and your budget. Avoid surprises, control the narrative and set the agenda.

When you lose control, life and work becomes very uncomfortable very fast. You find that you are offered more help than you want, someone else starts setting the agenda and you lose control of the narrative, which means that your efforts will not be portrayed in the best light. Being in control means being highly proactive. Make things happen, do not wait for things to happen to you.

Self-efficacy, locus of control and life prospects

The effect of self-efficacy and locus of control on longevity was demonstrated well by the two professors who came up with the ideas. At the time of writing, Albert Bandura (self-efficacy) was still going strong at age 92 while Julian Rotter (locus of control) died at the age of 98. They practised what they preached, and what they preach works. There is also a mountain of research that backs up their ideas.

If you want to live long and live well like the two professors, it makes sense to eat well, take exercise, avoid too much alcohol and even to keep on flossing. These are all worthy activities but they can be dull and boring disciplines which are easier to break than to keep. This matters not just from a personal perspective, but also from a public health perspective. Anything that can reduce the burden on over-stretched national health systems is probably a good thing.

But how do you make sure everyone flosses, let alone takes exercise and eats well? This was the challenge faced in Berlin, where they developed the BRAHMS programme,[52] which is a snappy way of describing the Berlin Risk Appraisal and Health Motivation Study. BRAHMS recruited 2,549 people to find out what drove health behaviour.

The project found that the single best predictor of sustaining these positive behaviours was self-efficacy:

- Sticking to a nutrition programme ($r = .34$).
- Sticking to an exercise programme ($r = .39$).
- Reducing alcohol ($r = -.28$).
- Frequency of flossing[53] ($r = .44$).

These results have been replicated consistently across countries and for all those health behaviours that are important but hard to sustain, including maintaining medications, practising safe sex and avoiding drug use.

This implies that diet books may be pointing in the wrong direction. They all try to find some miracle combination of foods that will quickly and easily let us lose weight. But the real magic is not in the recipes in each diet book: the magic key lies in how you think. If you think the right way, any sensible diet will work. If you think the wrong way, then no amount of diet books will save you from your waistline.

"If you think the right way, any sensible diet will work."

How locus of control may save your life

On one floor of a nursing home,[54] the residents were given maximum care: everything that could be done for them was done for them. They did not have to make any decisions for themselves and did not have to worry about anything. What's not to like about that?

The residents on another floor of the nursing home were given a different deal. They were given the freedom to arrange the furniture as they wanted, to come and go when they wanted. They were given the option of caring for a pot plant and they were encouraged to look after themselves as much as they could.

Which deal would you prefer? Be looked after in every way or have the freedom and responsibility to look after yourself as much as you can? If you choose freedom and responsibility, you will be twice as likely to survive. That is how powerful it is to feel a sense of control. The high-care group learned helplessness and dependence in a self-fulfilling way: the less they did, the less they became capable of doing until they could do nothing. The lower-care group stayed relatively active both physically and mentally. This finding is so strong and so consistent that standard practice in nursing homes is now changing: residents are encouraged to take as much care of themselves as possible.

Locus of control also has a surprising impact on your emotional wellbeing. It is easy to go through a normal day and feel a whole range of positive and negative emotions, depending on what is happening and who you are dealing with. But when that happens, you are letting your emotions be dictated to you by external events and other people. You become a victim of the world – and the world has no great interest in your wellbeing. As you saw in the last chapter, on using the power of emotions, you always have a choice about how you want to feel: your emotional state is your choice, not someone else's. To understand this, and to be able to act on it, is a very strong form of locus of control. You do not have to let other people control your feelings.

If locus of control and self-efficacy is simply a matter of trying harder, having self-discipline or showing some willpower or motivation, then that does not help at all. You cannot shout at people and tell them they have to try harder to stick to the diet. You need a way of nurturing self-efficacy and locus of control, so that all these positive behaviours become easy to acquire.

As you build self-efficacy, the result is a significant change in how you behave. As ever, behaviour patterns are just symptoms of thought patterns. If you fix your thoughts, you fix your behaviour. It is all in the mind. The behavioural symptoms of high self-efficacy are:

- You will take on more challenging tasks (you will take on the diet, not defer it).
- You will put in more effort to achieve your goal.
- You will stick at your task for longer.
- You will accomplish more.

These are highly resilient sorts of behaviour, which are well worth acquiring both professionally and personally. As with all habits of mind, these habits can be learned. The rest of this chapter gives you four practical exercises for building your self-efficacy and locus of control.

Cultivate the habit of self-efficacy and locus of control

The first step in cultivating helpful habits of mind is to know that you have a choice about how you think and about your habits. For instance, with locus of control you can choose to be like Hamlet:

> There is a divinity that shapes our ends
>
> Rough hew them how we may[55]

Hamlet was saying, in effect, that he was a victim of fate. Alternatively, you can choose to defy fate and follow the words of Nelson Mandela's favourite poem *Invictus*,[56] which sustained him through his many years of incarceration on Robben Island:

> I am the master of my fate
>
> I am the captain of my soul

These two poems echo the debate of the Reformation: are our fates all predestined for us (Catholic tradition) or do we have the free will to determine our fate (Protestants)?[57] At work, the smart choice is to stay in control. That is easier said than done. The following four exercises will help you make the right choice work for you:

1. Strive for mastery.
2. Deal with setbacks: watch the movie (not the snapshot).
3. Reach out.
4. Build influence.

Strive for mastery

Imagine that you decide to start learning the piano and, on day one, your teacher presents you with the task of playing Rachmaninoff's Piano Concerto No. 3, which professionals rate as one of the hardest pieces composed for piano. No amount of motivation or inspiration will help you play it. You will, in all probability, give up and look for another teacher. Your next teacher is more helpful. She starts by showing you how to hold your hands and gets you to play a simple scale: C major. The problem is that she never lets you progress: 30 lessons later, you are still playing the C major scale, and nothing else. You would rightly give up your second piano teacher and you might contemplate playing the banjo instead. You want mastery in the long term, and you want progress in the short term.

Mastery and resilience march together. We find it easier to sustain effort if we are good at something: top conductors keep going well past the age most people retire. Conductors are often addressed as 'maestro' for a good reason: they are masters and teachers of their art.

"Mastery and resilience march together."

Telling someone that resilience comes from mastery is like telling them wealth comes from having lots of money: it is true and unhelpful in equal proportions. It is unhelpful for two reasons. First, it raises the question of how to achieve mastery. If you lack mastery, does that mean you will lack resilience in the meantime? And, if you lack resilience, can you ever achieve mastery? Catch-22.

The second, and deeper, problem is that mastery by itself leads to brittle resilience: you will appear to have huge resilience, but your resilience will be very specific to the one area where you are expert.

Teach First[58] discovered the problem of brittle resilience in its early years. We successfully recruited outstanding graduates to join the scheme. The graduates were not just smart, they also had remarkable track records of achievement beyond the classroom as well. They had track records of more or less unbroken success: they could succeed at anything. They seemed to be the right stuff for taking on the challenge of teaching in some of the toughest inner city secondary schools. Towards the end of the first term, a tidal wave of crises hit the scheme. Graduate after graduate reported that they were really struggling, and they were on the brink of giving up. How could such successful people want to give up so easily?

The graduates all suffered the brittle resilience problem. Their success was their problem: they had never failed in life. They had no idea how to cope with failure or how to deal with real setbacks. As they struggled to teach and struggled to control their classrooms, they experienced lack of mastery for the first time in their lives. They no longer saw themselves as successful people, they saw themselves as complete failures. They could only see a bleak future.

The problem for the Teach First teachers is that they had been asked to do the teaching equivalent of playing Rachmaninoff's Piano Concerto No. 3, with just six weeks of training to prepare them. It was brutal, and they were set up to struggle. But they were not set up to cope with struggling.

Mastery by itself leads to brittle resilience: you succeed, but you cannot cope with adversity. The problem of brittle resilience suggests the solution: the journey to mastery matters as much as the destination. Achieving mastery is good, but what really matters is how you get there.

Your mastery to journey is best taken in small steps. We are all incompetent at anything we try the first time, from speaking a foreign language to learning how to play the piano or to teach. Watching an infant trying to walk for the first time is a humbling lesson in just how difficult anything is the first time you try it.

The mastery journey is covered in depth in the chapter on growth (Chapter 9). There, you will see how the Royal Marine Commandos are able to do a 30-mile self-directed march over the moors in the middle of winter with a pack weighing up to 60kg in less than eight hours. That is a superhuman effort, but it all starts 18 months earlier with a simple exercise: jog 2 miles in 22 minutes with no pack. Exercise 15 summarises the keys to a successful learning journey.

Exercise 15: build mastery

Building mastery is a long journey, but every mastery journey is based on three principles that you should follow:

1. **Incremental gains:** Start with small steps, and keep taking small steps. Keep pushing beyond your comfort zones, but avoid huge risk-taking which may result in triumph but is more likely to result in disaster.
2. **Smart gains:** Directed and purposeful learning beats brute effort every time. Use a coach, expert, trainer or mentor who can help you direct your learning and ensure your practice is deliberate and effective. Do not try to do it all yourself.
3. **Steady gains:** Practice and persistence pays. Keep repeating and reinforcing your learning. But make sure you follow steps one and two as well, otherwise persistence will not deliver progress. You want to have ten years of experience, not one year of experience repeated ten times.

Now look at how you are developing in your career. Are the projects and work you take on meeting the three principles of mastery above? If they are, you are probably growing your career. If not, you may be stagnating.

Portraits of resilience: self-efficacy

Roderic Yapp, Royal Marine Commando

The MV Montecristo had been hijacked in the Indian Ocean and the pirates were trying to burn the crew out of their safe room. Roderic had the task of boarding the ship, releasing the crew and seizing the pirates. This would not be a good moment to doubt yourself. Roderic had no doubts, nor did his team. Very quickly the pirates discovered doubt and surrendered: they preferred life to death.

Roderic's self-efficacy in the moment did not spring from nowhere. It was built on 15 months[59] of initial officer training: assault courses, brutal marches with 60kg packs across the moors, capsize drills in freezing water and long exercises with sleep deprivation on frozen hills or hot and humid jungle. Officers do the same exercises as other ranks, but faster: they visibly earn the right to lead. The training is not just about toughness: it is about building a toolkit of skills to help them make good decisions under pressure and in unfamiliar circumstances.

But however self-reliant you may be, Roderic is clear that success is a team effort (reaching out in Chapter 5). Teamwork is drilled into the Marines: many exercises cannot be completed unless the whole team works together. "You develop strong relationships: pressure bonds people. It is very cohesive, very direct. There is no bullshit, you cannot afford it." 'Humour in the face of adversity' is a core Marines value which binds the team. "Laughter is very serious," agreed Roderic, before recounting unrepeatable examples of Marine humour.

To survive 15 months of training, Roderic learned to manage his energy well (Chapter 6) by reducing each phase of training into short-term goals and by visualising his long-term goal (Chapter 7): "I could see myself passing out (graduating) on the parade ground with the Commando flashes. There was no going back: I had no answers to what I would do if I failed."

Deal with setbacks: watch the movie (not the snapshot)

Achieving mastery is a long journey, on which there will always be setbacks. It pays to know how to deal with these difficult times.

We all have moments where the world seems to conspire against us and disaster ensues. Looking at the snapshot of the disaster only makes things worse: you see just how bad things are, and it is hard to see any escape. It is very easy to start ruminating on how bad things are, how unfair colleagues, fate and the world are. From there, it is easy to start catastrophising about the future, which will look very bleak. These are moments when you need a different way of seeing the world. Instead of looking at the snapshot of disaster, watch the movie of progress.

In the early days of Teach First, many high-flying graduates faced a moment of truth when their world seemed to collapse around them. For instance, Emma[60] was a Teach First teacher who had graduated from Oxford University and was teaching science in north London. After just six weeks' training, she was posted to a very challenging school: over 60 foreign languages were used by students as their mother tongue, there were many first-generation immigrants for whom English was a second language, and the area scored highly on most indicators of deprivation such as poverty, single parents, poor housing, drug abuse and crime.

"Instead of looking at the snapshot of disaster, watch the movie of progress."

Inevitably, her first term was a challenge as she was learning the basics of teaching. Then she had the nightmare day. It all went wrong. The school principal decided to do a classroom observation. The principal chose the class with the worst behaviour. At the start of the class, three children decided to climb out of the window in a show of spectacular defiance. At the end of the class, after the other children had left, she did what any reasonable person would do: she sat down and cried. She had reached the end. She had just been humiliated by some 15-year-olds in front of the principal, and there was no way back for her. She couldn't teach and she couldn't even control her classroom. She gave herself an F for failure, for the first time in her life. At least, that was the way she saw it.

The principal saw it differently. The principal did not look at the snapshot, which was ugly. She looked at the movie, which was encouraging. This is a powerful way to look at events when things look bleak. The snapshot showed teenagers climbing out of the window and chaos in the classroom. The movie showed a young graduate making remarkable progress in a very short amount of time, but with occasional crises and disasters on the way. That is the nature of any movie: there are always crises on the way before the successful ending for the hero or heroine.

The principal took Emma back to her office, where Emma expected to get fired. Instead, the principal made tea. Tea is the leader's secret weapon: tea (or coffee) is a wonderful way of calming situations down and making difficult conversations easy. The principal got Emma to look at the movie, not the snapshot. In particular, she got Emma to recall successful lessons. The principal ignored the problem of the children climbing out of the window (for the moment). Instead, she asked Emma how she had managed to engage some children who had not been engaged with any sort of learning with any other teacher in the school.

"Tea is the leader's secret weapon."

By looking at the movie, not the snapshot, Emma changed her view of herself. She was not a total failure. She was a young graduate making rapid progress in very challenging circumstances, with occasional and inevitable setbacks. Looking at the movie of progress, not the snapshot of disaster, showed flexible, accurate and self-enhancing thinking. It then paved the way for a positive and productive discussion about how to control classroom behaviour better. What could have been a very difficult conversation for both Emma and the principal became a constructive discussion.

Everyone has moments like Emma had. You are having an 'Emma moment' when you find yourself catastrophising about your future and ruminating with regret about your present and past. Your snapshot of life will look ugly. That is the time to start looking at the movie and focus on the progress you have and will make.

Exercise 16: deal with setbacks

The road to mastery is rarely straight or simple. How you deal with setbacks is vital, because the difference between success and failure is often as simple as giving up or not giving up. When you hit a bump in a road, it helps to react positively. Here are three things you can do to frame your response appropriately:

- Look at the movie, not at the snapshot: focus on progress, not on setbacks.

- Focus on what you have done well: remind yourself that you can succeed.
- Focus on what you have learned: use setbacks as a source of strength and learning.

Ask these questions about some of your past setbacks. The chances are that, by asking these questions, you will be able to see how even setbacks can be helpful. This exercise works even better when you use it in real time on tomorrow's setback.

Reach out

Reaching out is a consistent theme of this book (see Chapter 5). This is for good reason: you cannot succeed alone, and we are all social animals. Reaching out matters professionally and personally. Reaching out helps build self-efficacy in three ways:

- professional support
- personal support
- power of role models.

"You cannot succeed alone."

Self-efficacy through mastery can only be achieved with professional support. If you want to master anything, from diving at the Olympics to teaching in an inner-city school to becoming an accountant, there is a craft skill that you need to master. For this, you need people who will guide you and help you. If you learn to play the piano, one of the first things you have to do is to learn how to hold your hands by the keyboard. It is not intuitive, and even if you consult Google or YouTube, all you find out is how you should do it.

You do not find out how you are doing it: you need a professional who can look at what you are doing and see the difference between what you do and what best practice looks like. Even top tennis players have coaches: the coach can see what is working and what is not working better than the player. The objective view makes all the difference.

Professional support can also help you with your learning journey. We have seen how Royal Marine Commandos develop from mediocrity to superhuman skills over 18 months. They undertake a carefully crafted learning journey in which skills, stamina and strength are built in endless small steps. The choreography of the learning is intense, and the rest days are a fundamental part of it. The learning journey has been honed over decades with thousands of recruits: the trainers at Lympstone know exactly how hard to push their recruits. There is no way a lay person could re-create that learning journey for themselves.

The Royal Marine Commandos also bake personal support into their training system.[61] Many exercises are designed so that they can only be achieved collectively: individual success depends on team success. They have a clear buddy system: buddies are meant to look out for each other, and check each other out for inspection, and to ensure their kit is in good order. Personal support is clear even in the mess room. If you want a cup of tea, be sure you ask everyone else if they want tea and then make it for them. Failure to do this and you are deemed to be 'jack': that is a real insult that marks you out as being selfish.

The drive for unity means that, unlike the rest of the armed forces, both officers and men undergo the same training regime at the same place: Lympstone. The only difference is that the officers have to perform most of the tasks faster. While the ranks have to do the 30-mile yomp over moors with their packs in 8 hours, the officers have to be able to do it in 7 hours. It would be interesting to see how many senior managers could perform the same tasks as their front-line workers, but faster and better.

You need your network of personal support. These are people you can rely on to encourage you, share a joke. They will listen to your triumphs and disasters and give you the emotional support we all need. They are unlikely to be the same people as those who can give you professional support, unless you have a coach who combines professional and personal support.

The third form of reaching out are role models. If we see someone else do something, then we are more likely to be able to do it ourselves. The trick is to find an accessible role model. If you see a top athlete or musician at their peak, it is inspiring but also daunting: the gap between what they do and what mortals can do is simply too great. An accessible role model is one of your peers who is perhaps a little way ahead of you. They show what you can realistically achieve. This is one of the reasons the officers train with the other ranks at Lympstone: the officers are highly accessible role models to the other ranks, because they are going through exactly the same training and they have to suffer just as much.

"Find an accessible role model."

Build influence

Achieving self-efficacy and locus of control at work is hard because you are not in control. As the world of command and control disappears, how can you maintain your locus of control? The chances are that you do not have all the resources you need to succeed, you are not in charge of making all the decisions about people and priorities and you have to cajole and persuade others to make things happen. It is not enough to manage your internal thoughts to achieve self-efficacy: you have to find a way of managing your environment as well.

We live in a world of work where you cannot control everything you want to control. You face three categories of activity, each with a different response:

- What you can control: make the most of these activities.
- What you can't control but influence: learn the art of influence.
- What you cannot control or influence: always have a Plan B.

The art of influence is the defining skill of twenty-first century management. It merits an entire book in its own right, and there is an entire book on it that I have written.[62] Note that persuasion is different from influence. If I persuade you to buy a car, which promptly breaks down, I have been persuasive but not influential.

Next time you see me, you will not want to hear me when I try to sell you a brilliant holiday timeshare deal. Persuasion is a one-off transaction, while influence is about building a relationship, or network of relationships, where you become a trusted partner to colleagues and customers alike. It is a work-based form of reaching out.

"Persuasion is a one-off transaction, while influence is about building a relationship."

Exercise 17: build your influence

At the risk of gross simplification, here are ten things you can do at work to be influential. Do all of this well, and you will maintain your locus of control and sense of self-efficacy. You will not become a victim of the world, because you can influence your world even if you do not have a reality distortion field to help you:

1. **Build trust:** always deliver on your commitments, find common ground with your colleagues – common interests, needs and priorities, make it easy for your colleagues – remove risks and obstacles to them working with you.
2. **Create loyal followers:** show you are genuinely interested in each member of your team and their careers, understand their needs, manage their expectations, build trust by having difficult conversations positively and early and always deliver on your commitments to them.
3. **Focus on outcomes:** work to clear goals that have visibility and impact across the organisation.
4. **Take control:** Have a clear plan for your department, know what will be different as a result of your work, build the right team and get the right budget and support for your plan. Do not accept the plan, team and budget that you inherit as sacrosanct.

5. **Pick your battles:** only fight when there is a prize worth fighting for, only fight when you know you will win and only fight when there is no other way of achieving your goal. It is better to win a friend than it is to win an argument.
6. **Manage decisions:** understand the rational decision (what is the best cost, risk–benefit trade-off?), manage the politics (what will the CEO and power brokers expect?) and the emotional decision (what do I feel most confident about and what will my team feel committed to?).
7. **Act the part:** act like other influential people in your organisation, be positive, confident and assertive and act like a peer to senior staff, not like their bag carrier.
8. **Be selectively unreasonable:** dare to stretch yourself, your team and others, make a difference by going beyond business as usual and beyond the comfort zone. This lets you learn, make an impact and build influence.
9. **Embrace ambiguity:** crises and uncertainty are wonderful opportunities to make a mark, take control and fill the void of uncertainty and doubt that others create. Ambiguity lets leaders flourish.
10. **Use it or lose it:** control your destiny or someone else will. You only remain influential if you use your influence.

Summary

Self-belief is a combination of:

- self-efficacy: believe you can achieve your goals in the face of adversity and
- locus of control: believe you can control your destiny and that you are not a victim of fate.

These are vital beliefs in the twenty-first century workplace: managers no longer just communicate orders and information up and down the hierarchy. You have to make things happen in a volatile, uncertain, complex and ambiguous world. They are also vital beliefs for your health and wellbeing: these beliefs mean you are more likely to stick to diets and medication and to take responsibility for your health. At work, these beliefs mean you are more likely to set yourself challenging goals and persist in achieving them.

Everyone has these beliefs to some extent. You can reinforce them in four ways:

1. Strive for mastery. It is easier to sustain effort where you are competent, not incompetent. Build mastery by making:
   - incremental gains: keep stretching yourself, but not so much that you break
   - smart gains: directed and purposeful practice is vital so get training, help and a coach
   - steady gains: persistence and practice pays
2. Deal with setbacks: watch the movie (not the snapshot). When you have setbacks, do not focus on the setback (the snapshot). Focus on the progress you have achieved (the movie). Reinforce the belief that you can succeed.
3. Reach out. You need three sorts of reaching out:
   - professional support to help direct your training
   - personal support to provide encouragement
   - accessible role models who show you that success is possible.
4. Build influence. You cannot succeed alone at work. Build your networks of trusted support at all levels, build alliances and find common agendas, know when and how to fight your battles.

Chapter 5

Reach out: the power of connections and networks

Reaching out to a healthy network of support will help you:

- spread your burden and manage your workload
- achieve your goals more easily
- deal with tough times professionally and personally.

The first part of this chapter will show why these benefits are essentials, not luxuries. The second part will provide you with simple tools to help you reach out, including:

- Building trust
- Effective listening
- Appreciative responding

Why reaching out matters

How many productive working hours can you deliver every day, week after week and year after year? This matters, because a sign of a resilient worker is someone who can sustain productivity for long periods.

The American Bureau of Labor statistics looked at the average productive working time of office workers, and found that they were productive for just 2 hours and 53 minutes every day.[63] That just beat the 2 hours and 29 minutes they spend on the internet doing non-work activities. The Bureau assumed, heroically, that time spent in meetings was productive time.

This survey was not a one-off. A Harris poll found that, in large firms, workers are focused on their primary task for just 45% of the time.[64] None of this will be a surprise to anyone who works in an office. Lean manufacturing has transformed production lines on the factory floor, but lean techniques and TQM[65] are yet to touch the office where the ambiguity of work allows inefficiency to proliferate. If work is too ambiguous and variable to measure, it is too difficult to manage efficiently.

This is good news: you do not have to work every hour of every day to be more productive than your peers.

So how many productive hours can you deliver every day?

The answer is, of course, as many as are needed. There is no limit to how many hours you can deliver every day. If you are constrained by your own working day, you will struggle to be truly productive for more than five or six hours. But, as a leader and a manager, your job is not to do all the work yourself. Your job is to build a team to get the work done: that means you can deliver as many productive working hours as you need to achieve your goal.

At this point, managers often object. If you have a limited budget, that caps how many resources you can rely on. And since budgets are never enough for the job in hand, the inevitable result is over-work.

Changing 750 million lives with 2 cups of tea

Two of us sat at the table drinking tea. Sharath Jeevan outlined the challenge. The UN estimates that there are 750 million children at school but not learning. Sharath pinpointed the core of the problem: many teachers had lost their intrinsic motivation for teaching. If we could help these teachers rediscover their motivation, we could change the education and lives of 750 million children. How do you do that when your total resources are two people with two cups of tea?

The answer was to set up STIR Education.[66] We then raised some money and hired some staff. And then we went about finding out how to address the challenge. Slowly, we realised that the best way is to work closely with each education system: work with the ministers, officials and teachers all the way from top to bottom. Instead of relying on hiring 10,000 staff, we work with each education system and use its resources to deliver the programme.

We deliver thousands of productive working hours every day, but not by working harder ourselves. We raised money to hire a great team giving us control over direct resources. We work with governments to deliver the programme, giving us indirect control over much greater resources.

STIR now works with 10 million children and is seeing very positive effects.

"Leadership is a team sport."

As a leader, if you have a good idea, you need to find the support to make it happen. Either you can ask for direct resources in terms of money and budget, or you can gain indirect control of resources by working with suppliers, customers and partners to achieve your goals.

In the movies, the lone hero always saves the world. In reality, the lone hero is over-worked, over-stressed and under-performs. Leadership is no longer about the great hero who changes the course of history. Leadership is a team sport and one of your main jobs as a leader is to find and build the right team.

"The lone hero is over-worked, over-stressed and under-performs."

Achieve your goals more easily

In the past, reaching out meant telling your staff what to do. In the days of command and control, power and seniority marched hand in hand: the more senior you were, the more resources you could command. But command and control is slowly dying. Management used to be about making things happen through people you controlled. Now, managers make things happen through people they do not control, or do not want to be controlled. That is a revolution that changes everything.

If you can no longer tell people what to do, you have to learn a new set of skills to lead well. You need to learn how to influence and persuade, motivate, build alliances and networks of trust, promote your agenda, influence decisions and fight battles without creating enemies. This management revolution raises the performance bar and sorts the best managers from the rest very fast.

"Managers make things happen through people they do not control, or do not want to be controlled."

The management revolution is driven by three trends, which will continue:

- professionalisation
- specialisation
- globalisation.

Professionalisation

In 1940, the US Census Bureau found that just 4.6% of Americans aged over 25 had a bachelor's degree. That has now risen to 33.4% and is set to keep on rising.[67] It is a trend that is mirrored around the world. The good news is that professionals can do more, but they also demand more. If you manage a professional, you probably manage someone who does not like being managed and thinks that they could do your job better than you can. Managers have lost the coercive power they used to have in the days of the one company town. Professionals can move job if they see better prospects or a better manager elsewhere. Command and control are breaking down as an effective way of managing. Instead, managers have to learn to influence, persuade and motivate their teams.

Specialisation

In 1928, Henry Ford bought 14,000 square kilometres of Brazilian rain forest[68] and established Fordlandia. His goal was simple: he needed to secure a reliable supply of rubber for his cars. Even until the late twentieth century, many firms were like medieval walled cities: all that was needed to sustain them was contained within their walls. But this is hugely inefficient.

When Boots, a long-established UK pharmacist, was manufacturing its own paper, it found that it was costing twice as much as buying it from outside.[69] Specialists beat generalists on price and quality, and so the walls of the old firms have broken down as supply chains have become increasingly fragmented and specialised. As a leader today, you cannot control the resources you need to succeed: you have to influence and persuade suppliers, customers and partners outside your firm to help you achieve your goals.

Globalisation

Cross-border business is growing relentlessly. Trade is now the equivalent of 55% of global GDP, up from 25% in 1960.[70] Together with complex supply chains, globalisation means you rely on people to make the right decisions for you while you sleep, you cannot see them and they work in a different language and culture. This is a world where command and control cannot work. Reaching out for support across the world is a high order skill of influence and persuasion.

> **"Globalisation means you rely on people to make the right decisions for you while you sleep."**

Specialisation, professionalisation and globalisation means that you can no longer rely on command and control. You need to reach out effectively to colleagues and partners within and beyond your firm. That means learning the subtle arts of influence, persuasion, coalition-building, agenda management, dealing with conflict and politics. Twenty-first- century management is more challenging than ever.

Deal with tough times professionally and personally

Shakespeare wrote: "When sorrows come, they come not as single spies but in battalions."[71] There are times when everything seems to go wrong, and these are the times when we need the most help. Within firms, when things go wrong, we tend to get precisely the wrong sort of help from top management. As top management slowly panics, it starts demanding reports, answers, updates and information, all of which take time and all of which prevent you from dealing with the actual problem.

In good times, you will have plenty of allies. In hard times, when you need your allies, you will find they disappear. Failure is a very lonely place. This is nothing new. Machiavelli, writing his advice for rulers in Renaissance Italy, noted that:

> Men are ungrateful, fickle, false, cowardly, covetous, and as long as you succeed they are yours entirely; they will offer you their blood, property, life and children, when the need is far distant; but when danger approaches they turn against you.[72]

Machiavelli did not bother to say what he thought of women at the time.

> **"When times are hardest you need your friends and allies the most."**

It is when times are hardest you need your friends and allies the most: they can help you find solutions, they provide moral and emotional support and they can provide practical help such as offering fresh resources and political air cover. To quote Hamlet again from the famous "To be or not to be" speech:

> Whether 'tis nobler in the mind to suffer
>
> The slings and arrows of outrageous fortune,
>
> Or to take arms against a sea of troubles,
>
> And by opposing end them: to die.[73]

Hamlet asks himself whether he should just accept and suffer ill-fortune, or fight fortune and expect to die. He missed the third choice: get some help from his friends. If he had sought help, English literature would have missed out on one of its great tragedies.

Relationships matter not just professionally, but also personally. Good social networks matter. 'Good' involves quantity (having many connections) and quality (supportive as opposed to abusive relationships). Research shows that people with good social networks:[74]

- live longer
- are healthier: mental decline sets in later and is slower
- are happier: they self-report better life satisfaction

Good relationships are not just about receiving support; they are also about giving support. Further research[75] shows that providing social support is as beneficial as giving, proving the old adages that "What goes round, comes round" and "As you sow, so shall you reap."[76] Giving turns out to be a very good way of taking when it comes to good relationships.

"A strong team beats a lone hero every time."

Portraits of resilience: reaching out

Nick Clegg, former Deputy Prime Minister

For a few years, the politician Nick Clegg was the most unpopular person in Britain. He led a small party, the Liberal Democrats, into a coalition with the Conservatives to form a government that helped the UK recover from the great financial crisis. This meant he was hated by the left-wing media for selling out to the conservatives. He was hated by the right-wing media for stopping the government being sufficiently right wing. He was even hated by half of his own party for selling out on the purity of opposition, for the compromises of power. The attacks on him were relentless from all sides, and were highly personal. Looking back, the period seems to have been one of great stability compared to the chaos that has engulfed Brexit Britain.

So how do you survive when every day you are being pilloried in the press, on television and on social media? Despite all this pressure, Nick never once cracked and never lost his temper.

Nick learned the power of reaching out the hard way. When he started as Deputy Prime Minister, he had virtually no support from the civil service or his party. He had no team and, yet, in government all decisions migrate upwards. He was buried in reviewing and challenging a mountain of decisions across the whole of government. His first task was to force the civil service to give him a team which took much of the burden from him. A strong team beats a lone hero every time.

His second secret of survival was a very strong network of family and friends outside politics. This is unusual: most politicians in Westminster live in a bubble where all of their personal and professional life is political. This gave him respite and comfort from the incessant personal attacks. It also meant he was not a prisoner of politics: he gained perspective, balance and options. When he left government and all the trappings of power, he simply went home and resumed his other life. Other leaders find it much harder to let go. He has since taken up a senior role at Facebook.

Reaching out was only part of Nick's resilience. He also had a deep belief that he could make a difference: he had a sense of purpose (Chapter 8) and self-efficacy (Chapter 4). He is also an optimist (Chapter 1): he sees government as helping make a better future. Finally, he learned to manage his energy well (Chapter 6). When things were really hard in spring 2011, he contracted pneumonia. After recovering from that, he hired a personal trainer, got more sleep, more exercise and a better diet. Deep challenge requires deep resilience.

What reaching out is and is not

The term 'reaching out' has notoriety in the world of work. It is a favourite phrase used by managers to imply that they have achieved consensus and support for an idea that needs approval, or for an initiative that they are about to impose. The quality of reaching out may be no more than an email asking for feedback: when none is received, that is taken as support for the idea. That is not reaching out in any meaningful sense, other than as a political device to push your agenda.

Reaching out in terms of resilience means two different things.

- **Professionally**: building networks of trust and support to make things happen.
- **Personally**: having friends and family who provide emotional support and relief from work.

These professional and personal networks are very different. Personal networks are about family and friendships. At work, networks are not about friends or family unless you work in a family firm.[77] Returning to Machiavelli, he asked a key question of leaders: "Whether it be better to be loved than feared or feared than loved?"[78] 500 years ago, the answer was clear: it is better to be feared. He then goes on to recommend a few executions to encourage everyone to keep the peace and stay loyal. This is not a choice open to managers today, although some are happy to resort to firing people to maintain their power.

> "Popularity is the high road to weakness in a leader."

Machiavelli was partly right: popularity is the high road to weakness in a leader. If you seek popularity, you will compromise on goals, you will avoid having the difficult conversations about performance and you will accept excuses for why things cannot be done on time. When you accept excuses, you accept failure. No amount of candy in a bowl by your desk will save you once you start accepting failure.

Machiavelli was only partly right, because neither fear nor popularity is the true currency of leadership, unless you are a politician or a dictator. The true currency of leadership is trust. And this is what your professional network is all about: you have to have a network of support built on trust and mutual interests.

"When you accept excuses, you accept failure."

Cultivate the habit of reaching out

As ever, it is easy to say that you should have deep and wide professional and personal networks, but it is not immediately obvious how you should do it. In this section, we will explore five practical techniques to help you build and sustain effective networks to support you professionally and personally. These techniques are:

- building trust
- listening to build understanding and relationships
- appreciative constructive responding: fix the roof while the sun shines
- gratitude: hunt the good stuff
- networking with purpose.

Building trust

Who wants to work with or live with someone they do not trust? Trust is at the heart of all good relationships. Making things happen within a firm depends on trust: negotiating a formal contract every time you ask a colleague to do something would cause the firm to go into gridlock. You have to trust your colleagues to do what they say. In doing so, you make yourself vulnerable. You depend on your colleagues to deliver, just as they depend on you to deliver. Trust, in the form of dependency and vulnerability, is the hallmark of any team. If you can do things without relying on others, then you do not need to be in a team.

Trust is the glue of relationships: it is the glue that holds firms together and is also the glue that holds society together. This trust is so deep we do not even realise we are depending on trust.

"Trust is the glue of relationships."

Deep trust

To see how far trust goes, find a dollar bill. On it you will find the words 'In God We Trust'. In practice, every dollar bill is a massive exercise in trust. We trust that a dirty, much used green piece of paper can be exchanged for goods and services worth \$1. If you draw a \$1 sign on another piece of green paper, it will be worth nothing – or possibly a small fortune. The artist Boggs made his career out of painting non-money, such as \$7 bills.[79] He made money by questioning the value of money.

Now the trust in money has gone so far that we can wave a piece of plastic at a machine and receive coffee or food in return. Money has become a massive exercise in social trust: money is worth it if we believe it is worth it. This allows for extraordinary experiments such as blockchain and quantitative easing[80] to come into existence. The moment society loses trust in money is the moment society implodes.

Building trust is an extended effort, and this is an extended exercise. You cannot say to people "trust me" unless you want to sound like a second-hand car salesman. In practice, trust is a function of four variables that you can manage. These variables are caught in the trust equation:

$$t = \frac{a \times c \times s}{r}$$

In the trust equation, where t = trust, each variable stands for:

- a: alignment of values and goals
- c: credibility
- s: selflessness
- r: risk.

Let's look at how you can use each of these four variables to build and manage trust.

Alignment

We all like to deal with people like ourselves. This is bad for diversity but good for efficiency. If we share common backgrounds, beliefs and ways of thinking, it is much easier to communicate with each other. Shared experiences are part of shared values: if we have been to the same college, attended the same conference and been on similar holidays, we start to have common interests. The power of shared experiences is vital: the corporate entertainment industry is built partly on this need. Taking time to chat about non-business matters when meeting for the first time is a good way to start building values alignment by finding where you have shared experiences and backgrounds.

Alignment is professional as well as personal. Once you have some measure of personal alignment, you can start to work on finding the professional alignment of goals as well. Professional alignment is about finding common goals and needs: this is the search for the famous win–win outcome in any negotiation, as illustrated below.

Personal and professional alignment

David ran the Middle East region of a fast-moving consumer goods company. He was very frustrated that his business partners seemed to want to spend their whole time chattering about life and family and other trivia. He could not understand why they did not get on with the job at hand: negotiating the next phase of the franchise development. His local partners could not understand David at all. They were trying to engage with him to understand him personally. Tarek turned to me and said: "How can we do business with someone we do not trust? How do I know I can trust him?"

David was focused on negotiating the contract and had faith in the contract. Faith in the law and in contracts makes sense in some countries, not in others. Tarek and his partners had no faith in contracts or in the law. They wanted to work on the basis of trust. Personal relationships matter.

Although David struggled to build personal alignment, he excelled at building professional alignment. He wanted to raise the franchise fees for his partners, sustain investment and beat competition. The franchises were deeply suspicious: they thought that he just wanted an excuse to squeeze them. Eventually, he was able to show to them that the increased investment would let them make more money, and that failure to invest would lose them money because competition would grow. This was classic negotiation: the win–lose proposition of a price increase was converted into a win–win of increased profit via increased investment paid for by the price rise.

Eventually, the logic of shared professional goals worked. He later confessed that he could have saved himself months of time and grief if the personal trust had been there as well.

> **"We judge ourselves by our intentions and others by what they do."**

Credibility

Friendships are based on personal alignment. But business relationships need the added ingredient of credibility. There is no point in working with people who cannot do what they say. Inevitably, we all think that we do what we say. The problem is rarely in what we do, because professionals always strive to do their best. The real problem is that we judge ourselves by our intentions and others by what they do. There is often a huge gap between what we say (our intentions) and what is heard.

For instance, when faced with a tricky request, we might say: "I will do my best ... I will see what can be done ... I will look into it ... It may be possible ..." What we say and what is heard is completely different. What is heard is: "I will do it." Two weeks later, we can come back and say: "I tried my best, I looked into it but sadly it cannot be done."

We know that we will have done as we have said. But the other party will feel very let down, especially if they were depending on us. Our credibility will be broken like a shattered vase. Broken trust, like a broken vase, is very hard to put back together again. The inevitable argument about who really said what, and what they really meant will do nothing to repair the damage.

Credibility starts with what you say. Be crystal clear about your commitments. It is far better to have a difficult conversation about expectations at the start than to have an impossible discussion about outcomes after the event.

Selflessness

When people are in it for themselves, it shows and we know it. We may have to deal with such people, but our dealings will be purely transactional. There is no basis of trust with selfish people. Selfless people are easy to trust. James Kelly, the head of a global consulting practice[81] was in a high-stress, highly demanding job. But he always found time to listen to team members and clients alike: he was instantly trusted by both. Giving is a good way of receiving: when you give your time or your support for free, the vast majority of people feel obliged to reciprocate. But there is a catch: give away too much for free and you devalue yourself. Soon, people take you for granted and exploit you.

Selflessness at work is not unlimited: where there is no reciprocity, the other side is being selfish. Both sides need to be selfless: this is the tit for tat principle. And this is how James Kelly worked: everyone knew that they could use his time, but you soon learned to use his time well in order to keep his trust. If you abused his time, you would find it hard to get more time with him.

> "Giving is a good way of receiving."

Risk

Trust is not like a digital on/off switch. The amount of trust you need depends on the amount of risk involved. You might ask a stranger for directions to the nearest post office, but you would be unwise to trust the same person with your life savings. The greater the risk, the greater the trust you need between two people. In practice, this means you have to build trust in small steps. Simple things like answering an email promptly or doing someone a small favour is a quick way of building trust. If you are dealing with a high-risk proposition, such as the decision to commission a big ticket programme, you need to find a way to de-risk the decision for your counter party.

Here are some simple ways you can de-risk a risky proposition:

- **Borrow trust.** If your idea is endorsed by someone your counter party trusts, that goes far in de-risking an idea. At its simplest, no one opposes an idea the CEO backs. Make sure you have the right people supporting you. It is also why celebrity endorsements work in the mass market: "If the golf clubs are good enough for the champion, they must be good enough for me."
- **Break your proposal down into small steps.** Find small agreements and common interests. You do not have to ask for everything all at once. Find the one part of your proposal that is most relevant and helpful to the other party and focus on that first. Build agreement step by step.
- **Offer a trial period or test market.** The unconditional money-back guarantee is a powerful signal to buyers that they do not have to take a big risk. Even mattresses are now being sold with 100 days money-back guarantees: all the risk of taking the wrong decision is eliminated.
- **Increase the risk of the other options.** All risk is relative. This is a favourite of CEOs trying to sell their change programme, when no one really likes change. The CEO will create the 'burning platform' to prove that doing nothing will end in disaster and lost jobs. The risk of change suddenly seems better than the risk of losing your job.

Exercise 18: build trust

When you need to build trust, remember the trust equation:

$$t = \frac{a \times c \times s}{r}$$

This means:

- a: build alignment. Find common interests and a common goal.
- c: build credibility. Always do as you say, and take great care in what you say: make sure you have agreed clear and common expectations. Borrow credibility from credible or powerful people who are prepared to support your idea.
- s: be selfless and be prepared to give time, help and support at least on a tit for tat basis.
- r: reduce the perceived risk of going ahead. Break it down into simple steps and remove any personal risk or threat from your idea.

Listening to build understanding and relationships

All great leaders and salespeople have something in common: they have two ears and one mouth. And they use them in that proportion. To be a leader you do not need to be a great orator, you need to be a great listener. Listening is the secret that lets buyers talk themselves into buying from you, lets strangers convince themselves you are friends and lets lovers talk themselves into bed. It is a simple and wonderful way to build your network of influence and support.

Listening works for two reasons:

- It helps you understand the other person: what hopes and fears they have and how they think. Once you know what someone wants, it is far easier to find shared experiences, explore common ground and build the alignment that is one of the foundations of trust.
- It is a subtle and effective form of flattery in a time-starved world. Research shows there is no point at which flattery becomes counter-productive.[82] Even obviously insincere flattery works. This makes sense because we live in a world in which most colleagues lack time or interest in showing they care for us. As a result, it is hard to resist liking a colleague who seems to notice that you are, as you always suspected, a wonderful person. Listening flatters because it is a way of saying

to someone: "I think so highly of you that I want to invest my time in listening to you, your wit and wisdom and your views of the world."

"There is no point at which flattery becomes counter-productive."

Exercise 19: listen effectively

Good listening is not about waiting to speak, or thinking up a clever response. Listening is about understanding and it is highly active. Here are three things you can do to listen well:

- **Look at the person speaking.** Looking at your phone is plain rude, gazing out of the window into the middle distance as you concentrate on framing your next point is obvious and shows you are not interested in listening. When you focus on the person talking, you are more likely to hear what they say.
- **Ask smart questions.** This is always better than making smart points. Making a smart point invites an argument. Asking smart questions shows you are listening and drives towards understanding. Smart questions are normally open questions that cannot be answered with a yes or no. They are questions that start with how, what, where, when or why. Failing this, you can always use the coffee house gambit: watch how two people gossip and all it takes for one person to keep going is for the other to say "Really ... Aha ... No! ... like?" The smallest prompt is enough to keep the conversation flowing. In a business context, "Say more" is often all you need to say.
- **Paraphrase.** This is a powerful technique where you summarise back to the talker what you think she said in your own words. This shows that you have been listening, it confirms understanding and identifies any misunderstanding fast. It also helps you fix their key points in your own mind more clearly. It also stops the talker repeating themselves, because they know that their point has landed.

Appreciative construction responding: fix the roof while the sun shines

Appreciative constructive responding (ACR)[83] is a highly effective way of reaching out and building your network. It is a way of showing that you will be there for your colleagues not only when it rains, but also when it shines. How you react to good news matters as much as how you react to bad news. The simple message is that you should aim to react actively and constructively to colleagues, not passively and negatively. This is easy to say, but not easy to do. One example will make the point.

> "How you react to good news matters as much as how you react to bad news."

Imagine a situation where you have just sold a major new contract to an important client. You return to the office and tell a trusted colleague about your success. Here are some possible reactions from your colleague:

- "You did what? How on earth are we going to staff that? The client will go crazy if they cannot get the right team fast. Are you mad?" Active/destructive response. This is a good way to start an argument.
- "Oh yeah ... well done. Everyone seems to be getting sales now. Did you hear about Maria's huge success at MegaCorp? Everyone is really excited about that." Passive/destructive response. This is a good way to deflate enthusiasm.
- "Oh ... well done." (Looking at Twitter feed.) Passive/constructive response. This is totally deflating.

This is the time to put down your social media or vital report you are working on, and invest some time in your colleague. Use the good times to build a relationship that will work in hard times: fix the roof while the sun shines. Show real appreciation. If your colleague then feels like a million dollars, she will be grateful to you.

> "Use the good times to build a relationship which will work in hard times."

Exercise 20: practise appreciative constructive responding

Deploy this exercise when someone comes to you with good news. It is your chance to build your relationship at warp speed. This is a simple exercise where the less you do, the better. ACR is a two-step process:

1. Focus on the person. Set aside whatever you are doing and focus on them and their success.
2. Explore the situation. Let them relive the experience in some detail: ask about the who, what, where, when. Ask what it felt like. Find out why it was a success and what worked well. All you have to do is to ask questions and let them do all the talking.

All of this is intensely flattering because you are showing deep interest in their success and you are giving them permission to relive their success. It is flattery where you never need to flatter explicitly: you do not need to say that it is the most impressive achievement since the building of the Great Wall of China. Simply letting them savour the moment is flattery enough.

ACR is also a good way of quietly coaching the other person. By exploring what went well, you help them identify what they were doing right and how they can sustain their success.

ACR is summarised in Figure 5.1.

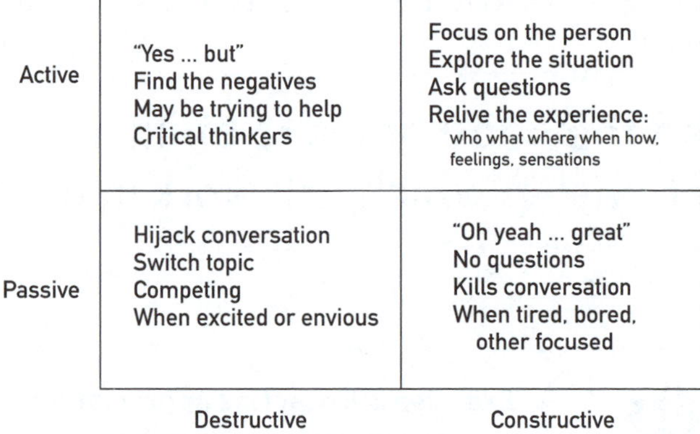

Figure 5.1 Appreciative constructive responding

Gratitude: hunt the good stuff

Thank you is short and simple, and much under-used. So use it more and more and more. It is a very simple way to win friends and influence people.

We all crave praise and recognition, and yet we rarely receive it. And, in more or less any situation, colleagues will be doing something that is worthy of recognition, so why not recognise it?

John Timpson set up and ran a large chain of shoe repair shops. This is one of the less glamorous businesses in the world. Most shoe repair shops are little more than holes in the wall at underground stations. Staff are often on low pay. But the service is great and the business thrives. There are, of course, many ingredients in a successful business model, but one of Timpson's secret weapons is praise. Normally, when a boss does a site visit, the result is tension: faults will be found, questions will be asked and improvements will be required. Timpson takes a different approach. In the back of his car, he carries a large supply of small rewards. He makes an explicit point of praising ten times as often as he criticises. Once you have that mindset, you find that even the one in ten criticisms is not necessary: you find a way of helping instead of criticising.

By giving small rewards and big recognition, he has a workforce that remains motivated to work in less than perfect conditions. You can always find things to praise, even in a hole in the wall shop.

> "You can always find things to praise."

How not to say thank you

I was coaching the CEO and she had just seen a staff survey which showed discontent among her top team. I asked when she had last thanked a team member for their work. She looked at me as if I must be mad. Eventually, she decided to try this weird idea of saying thank you to people when they do something well or helpful. What could possibly go wrong with saying thank you?

One month later, I returned to an office in turmoil. I asked around to find out what was going on. It was a totally divided office between Amanda's favourites and the rest who felt completely frozen out. Everyone knew where they were in her pecking order. Amanda had taken to thanking and praising her favourites in public at regular intervals and was completely ignoring the other half of the team.

Be generous with your praise – to everyone.

Exercise 21: show gratitude

Take a moment to reflect on all the ways in which those around you have been helping you recently. Their help may be as simple as being reliable in delivering on commitments. You will find plenty to be grateful for. As you build your gratitude list, you will find you have many excuses to appreciate your colleagues, friends and family.

Next time you see those who have helped you, say thank you. This is a one-second exercise with lasting impact.

If you want to make this exercise even more powerful, explain why you are grateful and how they made a difference to you. Remember, there is no point at which flattery becomes counter-productive.

Networking with purpose

In the age of social media it is easy to think that more is better. More Twitter followers and more likes may be good for a regular dopamine hit, but it is not an effective network. An effective network is both professional and personal.

Your personal and social network matters because it can give you moral support when you need it, and it is an escape from the relentless pressure of work. Chapter 6 will explore just how important this alternative source of energy and recovery is to sustaining resilience over the years.

Professionally, you need a network of people you can trust to help make things happen. You can map this network on paper and see where you stand. You need the following:

- Power brokers who can give you political air cover, guide you to the right assignments and mentor you on challenges and opportunities.
- Partners inside and outside the organisation who you rely on to make things happen.
- Influencers who can advise you on how to make things happen, and can be advocates for you to the rest of the organisation. They often exist in staff roles such as HR and finance.
- Angels, vital people who exist outside your firm. Some can help you by coaching, some can give you an external perspective that will help you rise above the day-to-day noise of the firm. Some may be people who can find you a role in another firm if you need it or want it. These may well be ex-colleagues. Most industries are small and incestuous, so it pays to keep on good terms with ex-colleagues: you never know when they might be important to you.

Network power

Every start-up goes through a near death experience where you face the threat of not making payroll at the end of the month. Not all start-ups survive the experience. This is when you discover that cashflow is not some abstract accounting report but is the difference between survival and collapse. One of my new ventures was rapidly heading towards the cliff edge and was running out of cash.

I was on a long flight on other business, when I spotted an old colleague I had not seen for ten years. We had kept on good terms, so we started talking. It turned out that he was running the family office for a billionaire. By the end of the flight, the start-up had secured its largest second round investor and its immediate cashflow problems were over.

Never burn bridges: you never know when your network might work to save you.

Building your network relies on using the reaching out skills in this chapter: building trust, showing gratitude, listening and using active constructive responding. There is no magic. It is a matter of applying simple and consistent routines to build relationships with the people who will matter to you. These routines are as important in your personal relationships as they are in your professional relationships.

Exercise 22: network with purpose

You will occasionally have the chance to grow your network at networking events and conferences. The prospect of meeting a room full of strangers fills some people with joy, others with dread. Either way, you need a disciplined approach to a room full of 300 people unless you want to spend two hours talking to someone you will never see in your life again.

Your first step is to prepare. In a room of 300 people, there may be four or five people you really want to meet. Work through the guest list and identify who you will target. Ideally, find someone else who knows your target and can introduce you: a warm introduction always beats a cold approach. If you have to approach them cold, then flattery helps: compliment them on something they have done, said or written. Then get them to talk about their favourite subject, themselves. Once they have told you how wonderful they are, you can mention that you would love to meet them again to discuss a matter of mutual interest. With that, your job is done: no need to make your pitch for a job or investment in a crowded room. Leave that until later. Once you have made your key introductions, you can decide whether you want to enjoy meeting more strangers or if you want to leave.

Remember that networking is work, so make it work for you.

Summary

Reaching out supports resilience in three ways by:

- spreading your workload and reducing your burden
- enabling you to achieve your goals
- helping you through tough times professionally and personally.

You have to build your network of support one person at a time using four techniques.

1. Building trust through alignment, credibility and selflessness.
   - Personal alignment: find common experiences and background to draw on.
   - Professional alignment: find common needs and wants, find the win–win.
   - Credibility: always do as you say. Have difficult conversations about expectations early, not impossible conversations about outcomes later.
   - Selflessness: be generous, but do not let people take advantage of you. You cannot take unless you give as well.
   - Risk: the higher the risk, the more trust is required. Take risk out of situations where you can.

2. Active constructive responding.

   Respond actively and constructively to good news and bad news alike. Invest time in colleagues. Building relationships while the sun shines will help sustain the relationship when the rain starts to fall.

3. Listening.

   Listen actively by asking questions, focusing on the talker and asking smart questions instead of making smart points. Listening is a strong and subtle form of flattery, and helps you understand how to influence the other person positively. Like all good salespeople, listen twice as much as you talk.

4. Gratitude: hunt the good stuff.

   Thank you is greatly appreciated, much under-used and simple to say. So say it. Often. You should be able to praise at least ten times as much as you criticise.

You need both personal and professional networks of support to sustain you through good times and bad. Review your professional network to make sure you have the right balance of partners, power brokers, influencers and angels in your network. Your social media followers are no substitute for a trusted network of support who can help you when you need it.

Chapter
6

Recharge your batteries: the power of recovery

This chapter is about how you can sustain performance and feel good over each day, week and year for your whole career.

You will discover how to be more productive by working less but better: minimising distractions and taking systematic, not random, rest breaks.

You will find out how to manage your ups and downs of energy and performance: no one can sustain peak performance for ever. Sleep, diet, exercise and rest are key resources for you in the long term.

This chapter gives you some realistic tools and techniques to help you manage these vital resources.

Why this matters

The tyrant King of Syracuse, Hiero, had a problem. He suspected that the goldsmith who made his crown had cheated and used some base metal instead of gold inside the crown. He did not want to destroy the crown to find out, but how could he be certain that his crown was solid gold? This sort of thing matters if you are going to be a first-class tyrant. Hiero did what any nouveau riche king would do: he hired the rock star scientist of the day to find out. Archimedes duly set about the problem which was to measure the volume of a very irregular solid: the crown.

The Roman historian Vitruvius[84] wrote that as Archimedes got into his very full bath, water flooded out: he had displaced water.

Archimedes had the original Eureka moment when he realised he could then measure how much water was displaced in a regular measuring jug. The volume of water displaced by the crown would be the volume of the crown. That would tell him how much it should weigh if it was solid gold. Vitruvius records that Archimedes jumped out of the bath and ran naked through Syracuse shouting Eureka! (Greek for I've found it!). Various spoil sports have shown that this story is probably completely untrue (Vitruvius lived 200 years after Archimedes). But never let reality get in the way of a good story.

Archimedes' Eureka moment is exactly the same as Newton's apple moment.[85] Newton retold the story many times, probably with embellishments. But the essence was always the same. He was meandering in his garden pensively when he saw an apple fall (not on his head). His 1752 biographer, William Stukeley, takes up the story:

> The notion of gravitation came into his mind. Why should that apple always descend perpendicularly to the ground, thought he to himself, occasioned by the fall of an apple, as he sat in contemplative mood.
>
> Why should it not go sideways, or upwards? But constantly to the Earth's centre? Assuredly the reason is, that the Earth draws it. There must be a drawing power in matter. And the sum of the drawing power in the matter of the Earth must be in the Earth's centre, not in any side of the Earth.

The common factor between Archimedes and Newton is that they were both busily doing not very much. They were thinking, but they were not busy multi-tasking on social media while looking at the TV, checking email, preparing dinner and giving the kids some quality time. Activity is not the same as achievement. Sometimes, inactivity is the best way to creative achievement. Archimedes was not the first, or last, person to have a good idea in the bath or shower.

"Activity is not the same as achievement."

It now appears that neuroscience is catching up with reality and explaining why some of our best and most creative thinking comes when we are not busy.

Why we are creative in the bath

Our autonomic nervous system (ANS) controls our glands and cardiac muscles and is involuntary: it is an entirely reflexive response. It operates through the sympathetic and parasympathetic divisions.

The sympathetic division is the fight or flight reflex.[86] This is a very useful reflex to threats. Your body diverts energy from maintenance activity, such as digestion, and focuses it all on action. Your body gears up for action: your heart rate and blood pressure increase to be able to release energy fast, your muscles tense up to be able to release speed and strength, and your body releases cortisol and adrenalin to support your reactions. In this phase, your pupils will dilate, and your vision and hearing become much more focused on the immediate threat: other stimuli get shunted away. These reactions are useful when being chased by a lion, but it is less useful when dealing with stress in the office all day. It is a good way to feel stressed out and exhausted, because your body cannot sustain this sort of intensity for long periods.

The parasympathetic division of the ANS is your 'rest and digest' mode. You no longer focus entirely on response to a threat. As you relax, your mind can start to wander and make connections between all the thoughts you have been storing up. This is just the moment you might make a connection between water displacement, crowns, baths, weights and gold which you would never make when in fight or flight mode.

Different sorts of work require different responses: sometimes the sympathetic and sometimes the parasympathetic divisions will help you most. The challenge is to bring the right reaction to the party, and to maintain balance.

> "Professional careers are more or less tailor-made for burnout."

Resting and relaxing is not only important for clear and creative thinking, it is also vital for long-term perseverance. It is not possible to sustain high effort indefinitely. Unfortunately, professional careers are more or less tailor-made for burnout. There are five reasons why burnout is becoming an endemic problem for professionals. These are not about your personality: they are about the changing nature of work:

- **Ambiguous work:** professionals cannot measure success in how many tonnes of pig iron they have shifted in the day. It may be possible to measure quantity (how many hours worked, how many customers seen), but it is much harder to measure quality: how good was that presentation, phone call, meeting? Having unclear goals is a good way to encourage stress.
- **Professional pride:** professionals have pride in what they do and want to do their best. This is a toxic combination with work ambiguity, because there is always more that you could do if you just worked a little longer.
- **Peer group pressure:** professionals flock together, which means your peer group will all be heading down the same path to success, and burnout, at the same time. It is hard to leave at 5pm if the office culture is that an early day means leaving at 7pm.
- **Technology enables us to work 24/7:** this reinforces the problems of work ambiguity, professional pride, peer group pressure and boss pressure. No one actually works 24/7, but it is easy to feel on call 24/7. We may leave the office, but the office never leaves us. In the past, work and family/leisure were compartmentalised which enabled for downtime and recovery. Now work and leisure are co-mingled, which means we never truly have time to recharge.
- **Lack of control:** the workplace is becoming harsher. Employment is less secure and even within work we lack the power and resources that managers enjoyed in the past. You have to make things happen through people you may not control or do not want to be controlled by. And if the work itself is not fulfilling, or you have unsupportive colleagues, your stress will be even greater.

The road to burnout is taken one small step at a time. It starts by checking emails late in the evening, then taking a few phone calls over the weekend, then staying late at the office each night, and then missing weekends to meet deadlines, and finally forgoing holidays and family weddings to meet vital work commitments that you will entirely forget in ten years' time. It is a drip, drip, drip process which happens easily. It is easy to miss the signs until it is too late.

The Mayo Clinic provides a useful checklist to spot the signs early, which I have adapted here:[87]

1. Are you becoming more grumpy, critical and cynical than normal?
2. Do you feel less energy? Do you have to drag yourself into work?
3. Are you using more alcohol, drugs, energy drinks than in the past?
4. Do you have trouble sleeping? Has your appetite changed?
5. Do small things and minor interactions irritate you more easily?
6. Are you suffering more minor physical ailments, such as headaches and backache?
7. Do you feel more negative about work, colleagues and your achievements?

As ever when you read a medical dictionary, the inevitable conclusion is to discover that you have symptoms of every mental and physical ailment known to science. So it is natural to experience some of the symptoms above from time to time: the fundamental ailment we all suffer is called 'life'. The question is how far these symptoms deviate from your normal state: the further you are from normality, the more the warning signs should start to flash amber or red.

"The fundamental ailment we all suffer is called 'life'."

Everyone is likely to experience burnout at some stage of their careers. 95% of HR professionals report that burnout is sabotaging their staff retention plans.[88] At any one time, 39% of employees report that they feel stress at work.[89] Stress is normally a reliable harbinger of burnout.

Managing your energy over the day, month and years is vital to sustaining performance and to persevering to succeed. The energy grid table below is a way of mapping how you can manage your energy.

The energy grid

	Negative emotions	Positive emotions
High energy	*Survival zone* *Aggression* Stressed, anxious Focused Assertive, aggressive	*Performance zone* *Passion* Excited, hopeful Engaged, committed Positive, optimistic Committed
Low energy	*Burnout zone* *Resignation* Disillusioned Tired, low energy Cynical, grumpy, negative Bored	*Comfort zone* *Recovery* Relaxed, calm Happy, positive Sociable Creative

Clearly, we would all like to be in the performance zone all the time. But this is simply not possible for two reasons.

First, there will be occasions when we face adversity and our positive emotions turn negative. In sports, both teams may start out in the positive zone and feel excited, energetic and optimistic about their prospects. But then one team falls behind: at that point, many players switch from the performance zone to the survival zone. They need to find a way out of their predicament, and the clock is ticking: that is real pressure.

The same happens at work. When things are going well, it is easy to feel that you are in the performance zone. But there is a limitless supply of crises and conflicts at work that can tip you into survival mode at speed. These may be momentary crises, or they may be more pervasive career crises which can cloud your outlook for months or even years at a time.

You can still perform well, sometimes very well, in the survival zone. And, as a professional, you are probably committed to doing the best job possible in even the toughest circumstances. But there is only so long that anyone can fight against the "slings and arrows of outrageous fortune".[90] There is a natural progression from survival to burnout: the better progression is from survival to recovery.

The second reason why we cannot sustain the performance zone indefinitely is that we need time to recover occasionally. Recovery and downtime are not a distraction from performance: they are a vital part of sustaining high performance. All top athletes have regular rest days, not because they are idle but because rest improves performance.

"Rest improves performance."

The rest of this chapter will show how you can manage your energy effectively across the day, a month and a career.

Cultivate the habit of managing your energy to sustain high performance

Manage your daily routine to maximise your energy

The importance of day-to-day energy management was first docu-ment by Frederick Taylor, the godfather of Scientific Management. This means he was widely hated during the twentieth century by workers and unions alike, because he was also the godfather of time and motion studies which squeezed maximum productivity out of workers. It is safe to say that he was not the worker's best friend. His attitude to workers can be summarised in his description of labourers who had the job of moving pig iron:

> One of the very first requirements for a man who is fit to handle pig iron as a regular occupation is that he shall be so stupid and so phlegmatic that he more nearly resembles in his mental make-up the

> ox than any other type. The man who is mentally alert and intelligent is for this very reason entirely unsuited to what would, for him, be the grinding monotony of work of this character.[91]

Taylor then set about raising the output of the men handling pig iron. On average, they could handle about 12 tonnes of pig iron a day per person. He identified one worker who he called Schmidt.[92] He then worked with Schmidt to raise his productivity so that he could shift 48 tonnes per shift, without exhaustion. That was a four-fold increase in productivity. The principles that Taylor used were very simple:

- Enforce rest breaks every hour, for about five minutes, even if Schmidt did not feel tired.
- Reduce the working day from 10 or 12 hours to 8.5 hours.
- Ensure the work was focused and efficient.

Taylor showed that more rest ensured more productivity every day. He had no interest in being nice to employees: he wanted to force as much productivity out of every dollar of wages he could. He found that the best way to do this was to work less, but to work better. You can use exactly the same principles of shifting pig iron to shifting work in the office.

Below are three positive exercises which draw on the lessons of Taylor and Scientific Management.

Exercise 23: take rest breaks

The goal of this exercise is to sustain high energy over your whole working day. The essence is to make sure you have frequent, if short, breaks in the day. Target taking five minutes off every hour, even if you do not feel tired. The break might be as simple as making a cup of coffee or chatting with a colleague.

These hourly breaks not only help your energy levels, they also help you focus on your work. Instead of facing eight hours of daily clashes, interruptions and conflicting goals, you can use each break to create a short 55-minute sprint for yourself. Each sprint can be deliberate and focused. Inevitably, some of your sprints will fail because of the random nature of office interruptions, but at least the breaks give you focus and structure to your day.

This is classic 'Short Interval Scheduling' and it helps with focus and efficiency. If you have a big task, split it into bite-sized pieces lasting less than an hour. Go all out to complete the first step of your task and then take a break: reward yourself with a trip to the coffee machine, or give yourself a quick dopamine hit by seeing how many people have liked the picture you posted on social media. As we saw with Schmidt, it is vital to take this break even if you don't feel tired. The quick recharging of your batteries will help sustain you through the next hour.

Use the same approach if you have a task you do not like much. If you have to make some cold calls, break the calls down into achievable targets. Set yourself the task of making the first five calls and then reward yourself with a quick break.

"Tiredness is as bad as drunkenness."

Exercise 24: reduce your working day

The goal of this exercise is to make sure that you deliver at least five hours of truly productive work per day, which is far more than most of your colleagues will achieve. To do this, be very clear about what you need to achieve in your day, week and month. This will let you focus on what matters (the signal) and not the noise. If you are unclear about what you must achieve, your whole day will be sucked into dealing with the day-to-day noise of office life.

If you are in a firm where long hours are seen as a job requirement, you can still focus on producing five stellar hours. You can use the rest of the time for networking, gossip and pointless meetings to fill the hours. You could even use the surplus time for some creative thinking.

If you have to put in long hours, avoid important work at the end of the day when you are tired. Tiredness is as bad as drunkenness. Working after 17 hours without sleep has the same effect as having a blood alcohol level of 0.05%: reaction times slow down by 50%.[93] Even Frederick Taylor recognised that shorter working days are more productive. The nations with some of the shortest working hours (Germany, Denmark, Norway and Luxembourg) also have some of the highest productivity and highest per capita incomes.[94]

Already, some firms are experimenting with a shorter working day and shorter working week, and they are finding it works. Jonathan Elliot, CEO of Collins SBA in Australia, found that he was most productive over five hours, and decided to move all his staff to a five-hour day and see what happened. To make it work, long meetings had to be ditched and replaced with ten-minute huddles. Everyone had to work more efficiently and there is less gossip than before. But the results are strong, sick days have plunged, good talent has been recruited and some advisors are achieving record results. They are keeping the experiment going.[95] Clearly, one successful experiment does not prove that this is the future of work, but it shows what is possible.

Exercise 25: ensure your work is focused and efficient

Inefficiency is baked into office work as much as efficiency is baked into work on the factory floor or in distribution and other easy-to-measure occupations. The three main drivers of inefficiency are ambiguity, interruptions and pointless activity. If you can tame these three productivity killers, you will have stellar productivity. Here is how you can make every hour an effective hour:

1. **Be clear about your goals.** Drive out ambiguity. This is the same message as Exercise 24, and it is worth repeating. Unclear goals and processes lead to rework and wasted time such as pointless meetings.

2. **Avoid distractions and interruptions.** Planned and unplanned interruptions are like kryptonite to productivity and performance. Avoid the distractions of email, just making a quick phone call, checking social media or having a gossip. When you work, work and be very clear about what you need to achieve. If you need to deal with the noise of email and phone calls, set aside brief periods when you can do this.

   An analysis[96] of 10,000 programming sessions recorded from 86 programmers using Eclipse and Visual Studio found that a programmer takes between 10 and 15 minutes to start editing code after resuming work from an interruption. If there are 15 interruptions a day, that is up to half the day lost. Interrupted work takes twice as long and has twice as many errors.

3. **Do one thing at a time.** You may imagine that you are being highly productive by multi-tasking, but you are not. Anyone who multi-tasks may look busy, but is busy achieving very little. Research[97] shows that the more complex or unfamiliar tasks are, the harder it is to switch between them. Productivity falls by up to 40% when you multi-task. And if you doubt how hard it is to multi-task, look at anyone who is trying to walk in the street while texting.

"Planned and unplanned interruptions are like kryptonite to productivity and performance."

These exercises are more or less the opposite of standard working culture in most offices: work long hours, deal with endless interruptions, multi-task, take erratic breaks when you can, and shift between work and personal activities. This working culture is a recipe for low productivity and low resilience. It means many people are working hard to shift 12 tonnes of the office equivalent of pig iron, while they could be shifting 48 tonnes with more focused effort and energy.

It is better to work smart than to work long.

Manage your energy for the long term: be kind to your body

Sustaining effort over each and every week needs different techniques from sustaining effort during a single working week. There are four routines that will help you last the course, month after month after month:

- Use the power of recovery and rest.
- Sleep your way to success.
- Diet realistically, diet for life.
- Exercise to perform, not compete.

Use the power of recovery and rest

We take the seven-day week for granted. But it is a very unnatural amount of time: 4 weeks is only 28 days, which really messes with any lunar calendar that depends on months that are 29.5306 days long. The ancient Egyptians worshipped the sun, not the moon, so they settled for three ten-day weeks a month and added five days at the end of the year to regularise their year.[98] The French revolution, with its decimalisation craze, also introduced a ten-day week. It was Judaism that introduced the 7-day week over 3,000 years ago.

Within all these schemes was the idea that there should be one or more days of rest. The Romans had *nundinae* every eight days. These were market days and the plebs were excused work in the fields.[99] Emperor Constantine introduced Christianity and the seven-day week (following the Judaic tradition) in AD 321. He also made the seventh day a legal holiday.[100]

The importance of rest days has long been recognised. The Roman patricians were not trying to be nice to the plebs: they realised that rest days were a good way of keeping the plebs quiet and maximising their productivity. In similar fashion, Henry Ford introduced a five-day week at his car factories in 1926, at a time when a six-day week was standard practice. He found productivity was not affected. Gradually, the idea of the two-day weekend spread.

The idea of rest days run deep in history and across cultures for good reason: people need to rest to perform. A short examination of athletes' training logs show that rest days are built in. The Royal Marine Commandos's training programme has one rest day built in every week.[101] Rest days are vital to your physical and mental recovery.

> "Rest days are vital to your physical and mental recovery."

The cult of 24/7 working is deeply unhelpful. For most of us, it is a myth that is not true. OECD shows that the average working year is now 1,770 hours,[102] or 34 hours per week including holidays and sickness. That is nowhere near 24/7 working. In practice, you probably find the rush hour at 8am on a Sunday morning to lack any rush: most people are not going to work. But even if you do not work 24/7, the advent of technology means that it is hard to switch off.

Exercise 26: use the power of recovery and rest

This is a very simple exercise that calls on you to do nothing at all – at least once a week. It is an exercise that over-achieving multitaskers find more or less impossible to implement, but is vital to sustaining your energy in the long term. The lesson of history, and the lesson of all high-performing athletes, is that you need to rest once a week at least. You are not being idle, you are helping yourself sustain high performance.

Enjoy being idle, occasionally.

Portraits of resilience: manage your energy

Tor Garnett, Detective Superintendent in the Metropolitan Police

Tor is one of youngest detective superintendents in the Metropolitan Police, and has worked in highly demanding roles including counter terrorism. In popular imagination, there is good and bad. In practice, police work is more often dealing with chaotic situations and people. Tor explains: "You need a high tolerance of ambiguity. Nothing is black and white. You always operate on a grey scale. Nothing is simple." Police work is high stakes, highly demanding, highly ambiguous and 24/7 because crime never sleeps.

To maintain this tolerance of ambiguity, you have to manage your energy, which Tor tries to achieve by focusing on daily and weekly disciplines. She has sharply honed routines including: maintain a day book to ensure the right tasks are done at the right time, clear the big least favourite tasks at the start of each day then do all the meetings and the emails. In a good week she does high-intensity exercise three times a week, meditation three times a week and four minutes of yoga to start each morning. She manages a careful diet with protein for breakfast and always carries a bottle of water. She does no social media during the week, spends the final two hours of the week doing a 'weekly review' of progress and the plan ahead. Once every three months, she does a full stock take of how she can improve on what she is doing and how she does it. She tries to be highly intentional about everything she does, so that minimum effort is wasted.

This discipline has not come about by accident. Tor learned from mistakes and doing 'track downs' when things break down. Energy does not just sustain itself: it has to be nurtured. As with many leaders, she is highly focused on learning (Chapter 9), she reaches out (Chapter 5) professionally by investing in her team and personally in her social and church networks.

Sleep your way to success

Exercise 27: sleep well

Sleeping your way to success has a long and ignoble history, in which the key did not involve any actual sleep. You can make your own choices about that sort of sleep. The nature of this exercise is somewhat different and the message is simplicity itself: sleep more, sleep better.

Research shows that real sleep is the secret of success for many high performers. Sleep deprivation is a good way to achieve poor performance. Working long hours with minimal sleep is heroic and futile. Extensive research shows that most of your cognitive functions get worse with sleep deprivation, including:[103]

- attention
- working memory
- reaction speed
- reaction accuracy
- memory recall
- decision-making
- flexible thinking.

In other words, everything you need to function well will get worse with lack of sleep. In addition, we know from experience of colleagues and toddlers throwing tantrums that tiredness leads to grumpiness. A tired person not only thinks poorly, but also behaves poorly. That is not good for your performance at work or behind the wheel of a car. Roughly one in ten serious accidents involve a fatigued driver.[104] Roughly one in five fatal accidents involve a drowsy driver. Being tired can kill you and other people.

In contrast, plentiful sleep aids performance. In a simple experiment,[105] the Stanford University men's basketball team was put through an extended sleep exercise regime. They were given the target of a minimum ten hours in bed per night, which is far more than the seven or eight hours that most people manage. After seven weeks of the extended sleep regime, performance improved significantly:

- Sprint times improved by 4.4%.
- Free throw shooting accuracy improved by 9%.
- Three-point field goal percentage increased by 9.2%

"You really can sleep your way to success."

Given that many contests are decided by marginal differences, these are huge gains to make. It seems that you really can sleep your way to success.

Diet realistically, diet for life

Diet has taken a long time to be recognised as a key to performance. Early experiments in diet were dangerous in the extreme. The Tour de France has always been an extreme test of endurance. In its early days, it was also an extended experiment in doping, which was mainly used to help overcome the pain of the tour. The 1923 winner explained the horror of the tour in a book called *The Convicts of the Road.*[106]

> "You have no idea what the Tour de France is", Henri said. "It's a Calvary. Worse than that, because the road to the Cross has only 14 stations and ours has 15. We suffer from the start to the end. You want to know how we keep going? Here ..." He pulled a phial from his bag. "That's cocaine, for our eyes. This is chloroform, for our gums."

Cocaine and chloroform were just the starters. Amphetamine, alcohol and strychnine use was widespread. Some riders developed so much tolerance to strychnine that they were taking it in quantities that would kill most people.

While you might want to administer large doses of strychnine to some of your colleagues, this would be unwise. It is also no longer best practice to go into work on a diet of amphetamines, cocaine and alcohol.

The science of diet has moved on and it clearly affects cognitive performance as well as physical performance. Students, as ever, provide us with the evidence. From an experimenter's perspective, students are easy to study: their results are easy to compare and it is relatively easy to set up and run tests on students. The evidence is stark: better diet means better performance, by a long way. A test[107] of 395 16-year-old students in Santiago, Chile, looked at the link between diet and performance. The students' diets were assessed based on how much saturated fat, fibre, sugar and salt they ate. They were then divided into healthy, medium or unhealthy groups. The healthy students scored a grade point average (GPA) of 515, versus the unhealthy at 460.

The huge difference in GPA scores did not come from having some weird and wacky diet that is hard to sustain. The difference came mainly from avoiding junk: salt, sugar, saturated fat that you are likely to find in takeaways, processed foods, sweets, chips and other dangerous treats. Healthy foods include protein, fibre, fruit and vegetables. There is no great mystery to what a good diet looks like now: we have moved on from the Tour de France of 100 years ago.

But if eating the right type of food is hard during the working day, there is one other dietary secret that helps high performance: eat breakfast. Once again, students provide the evidence. Students who eat breakfast are more likely to:[108]

- achieve well academically
- behave well
- take exercise
- maintain a healthy weight.

A representative study of students in Abu Dhabi[109] showed that 51% of students who ate breakfast scored an A grade versus only 31% of students who skipped breakfast. In the UK, 70% of teachers report that breakfast clubs[110] improve student concentration, and 60% report improved behaviour, with only 1 to 2% reporting negative effects on concentration and behaviour. If you want to be an A grade player, breakfast makes the difference.

The resilient mindset for dieting includes self-efficacy – believing you can achieve your goals (Chapter 4), being positive and focusing on what you can do and eat, not on what you cannot do or eat (Chapter 1) and reaching out for positive support and role models to help you (Chapter 9).

Exercise 28: eat a high-performance diet

Most diets are hard to sustain because they make unusual demands on you. You do not need an extreme diet, you need a sustainable diet. Here are three keys to a high-performance diet. It may also have the side benefit of helping weight control:

- Reduce the amount of junk in your diet. The bad stuff is well known: saturated fats, sugar, salt and alcohol. You cannot avoid it completely, but you can reduce the bad stuff.

- Eat breakfast. Breakfast is your fuel for the day: starting the day without fuel is like starting a car without fuel. You will get nowhere fast. The old adage says: "Breakfast like a king, lunch like a prince and dine like a pauper." On this occasion, folklore is a good guide to behaviour. Breakfast makes a big difference to performance: it may also help control weight, although the evidence is less clear-cut.[111]
- Build the resilient mindset, especially around self-efficacy (Chapter 4). With the right mindset, any diet works. With the wrong mindset, even the best diet fails.

"Starting the day without fuel is like starting a car without fuel."

Exercise to perform, not compete

There is an emerging cult of the super-fit executive who claims that they do a triathlon every morning before starting work. Intense exercise is a sign of the competitive over-achiever who wants to win at everything. Fortunately, there is no evidence that extreme fitness leads to anything other than extreme fitness. It is also not consistent with the theme of this section: be kind to your body. But there is a link between exercise and sustaining high performance.

The importance of exercise was first noted by the godfather of medicine, Hippocrates, who gave the medical world the Hippocratic oath. In the days before big pharma, there was not much knowledge of medicine, apart from herbal remedies and vile concoctions of animal parts. For Hippocrates, the solution was clear: walking is the best medicine. 2,500 years later, modern medical practice may be catching up with Hippocrates: forget the triathlons, walking really is the best medicine. Just playing golf could reduce your mortality by 40% and give you five extra years of life, if you think playing golf is a penalty worth paying for five years more life.[112]

Neuroscience is starting to show that exercise affects aging and cognition. The surprise finding is that exercise results in neurogenesis.[113] Instead of a steady decay of neurons in the brain, exercise results in new neurons being generated, especially in the hippocampus. This helps sustain cognitive and memory performance as you age.[114] Armed with this knowledge, a large number of neuroscientists are also dedicated joggers. If you want the resilience to sustain performance in the long term, exercise makes the difference.

Exercise also has more immediate effects.[115] Aerobic exercise can do the following:

- improve mood
- enhance sleep
- reduce stress and anxiety
- improve creativity.

It also appears to improve cognitive performance at any age. Even among schoolchildren, a ten-minute workout improved maths test scores significantly on the day.[116] In the longer term, fitter children outperform less fit children significantly.[117]

If you need to find a creative solution to a sticky problem at work, do not sit and worry. Stand up and go out for a walk. Walking even improves creativity or 'divergent thinking'. Fortunately, it is possible to test and measure creativity. The simplest test is to see how many different uses you can think of for a paperclip,[118] or old shoes or any other common item. You might try this yourself. Your creativity is then measured against three factors:

- Fluency: how many ideas you can generate.
- Flexibility: the number of different types of uses.
- Originality: how uncommon your answers are.

A Stanford University study[119] found that 81% of people who walked improved their creativity while walking. As impressive, these participants remained more creative after they sat down again. Walking outside generated better quality of creativity than walking on a treadmill. Once again, modern science is proving Hippocrates was right: walking is the best medicine.

"Walking is the best medicine."

Exercise 29: do some aerobic exercise

Fortunately, the exercise you need is both specific and modest. Aerobic exercise is best. Stretching, resistance training and muscle-toning exercises appear to have no effect. This is just as Hippocrates noted 2,500 years ago. That does not mean you have to buy some running shoes. It means making some simple adjustments to your daily life, such as:

- getting off the bus one stop away from your destination and walking the rest of the way
- walking up two flights of stairs instead of waiting for the lift
- walking to the local shops instead of driving there.

These are small adjustments to the daily routine which are easier to make than taking part in triathlons. You can also find plenty of other excuses during your day to walk a little more. Make walking a resilience habit. The more you do it, the more you will enjoy it.

Modest exercise will help you feel good and function well.

Summary

Recharging your batteries is vital to sustaining high performance over the short term (day to day) and long term (year after year). Inevitably, your energy will ebb and flow. We all want to be in the performance zone, but it is impossible to stay there all the time. When events conspire against you, you may well find yourself in the survival zone. This is also the danger zone. It is very easy to move from survival to burnout, but it is more or less impossible to go straight from survival to performance. Your best way out of the survival zone is to rest: go into recovery mode. Recharge your batteries and then you will be able to move back into your performance zone.

Day-to-day energy and performance management

Day to day you can manage your energy and sustain high performance by following the same rules that were used to produce a four-fold increase in labour productivity over 100 years ago:

- Take frequent rest breaks even if you do not feel tired. Use short interval scheduling to break big tasks into small tasks and then reward yourself when you complete each mini-task. Aim to break for five minutes every hour.
- Reduce your working day. Focus on delivering five stellar hours of work each day. Use the rest of the time for gossip, social media, networking and creative thinking. If you produce five hours of great work a day, you will be ahead of most of your colleagues.
- Stay focused and efficient, which is the key to your five stellar hours. Avoid distractions, planned or unplanned. Avoid multi-tasking which is how to do several things inefficiently and ineffectively at the same time. When you work, really work.

Long-term energy and performance management

- **Rest days:** elite athletes know the importance of recovery days. Throughout history, societies may have disagreed on the length of the week but they have all agreed on the importance of rest days each week. Working 24/7 is heroic and futile: you will burn out. Rest to perform.
- **Diet:** ditch the junk food, eat the good stuff: fruit, vegetables and protein. Your brain and body will thank you and give you improved performance in return. And eat breakfast: fuel your tank for the day ahead.
- **Sleep:** you can sleep your way to success. Lack of sleep leads to worse mental performance and worse social interaction.
- **Exercise:** the good news is that you do not need to be a gym bunny to exercise. You simply need to walk more because walking is the best medicine. It is good for both body and mind.

Exercise 30: manage your energy flows

Use the grid below to monitor and manage your energy over the short and long term. The good news is that you should not expect to be in the performance zone all the time. That is impossible to sustain. If you find yourself in the survival zone from time to time, that is part of life. Do not expect to be filled with positive emotions all the time: accept you will have to work through hard times occasionally.

The secret of this grid is to focus not on the obvious place, which is the performance zone. Instead, focus on the bottom right-hand corner: the recovery zone. Recovery periods are vital for all top performers, most obviously in sports. Recovery is vital if you have been in the survival zone. Recovery time is not idleness: it is about sustaining resilience and performance in the longer term.

Resilience is not about heroically keeping going in the face of all the odds. It is about working smart, not hard. That means being kind to your body and sustaining the energy to perform both short term and long term.

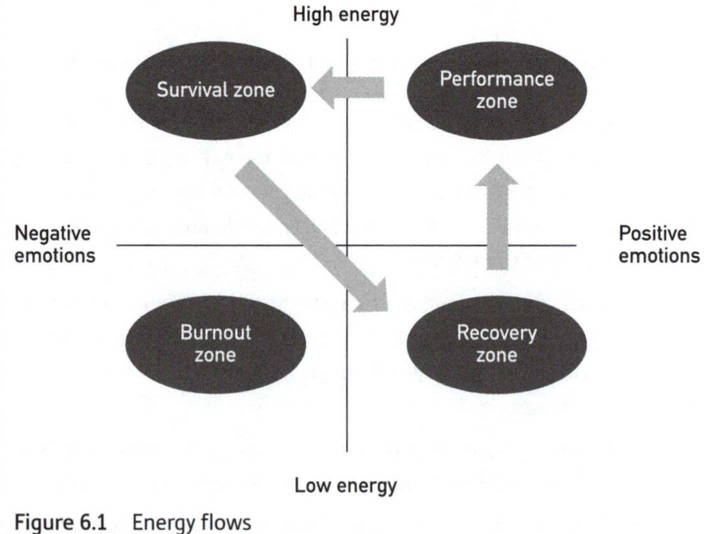

Figure 6.1 Energy flows

Chapter
7

Stay mindful: the power of choice

This chapter is about managing the 1% of your time that is the high adrenaline, make or break moments of your career. Resilience is not just about managing adversity and persevering for the long haul. This chapter will help you make the right choices in real time and turn crises into opportunity.

Why it matters

There is an old adage that war is 99% boredom and 1% terror.[120] That might equally apply to a career, or even to life. 99% of the time we cruise on autopilot. But 1% of the time is pure adrenalin. These are the moments of crisis and conflict that define your career. They are the moments when reputations are made or lost and power visibly shifts from one person to another. Some of these moments are planned, others are unplanned. For instance:

- At the job interview, you are asked a provocative and potentially offensive question. How do you respond?
- A crisis emerges and no one is sure what to do, but you have an idea. Do you take a risk and step up or play it safe and step back?
- In the meeting, the accusations start to fly. Do you fight, freeze or flee?
- Your boss tries to bully you into taking on an assignment you do not like. Do you fold or not?
- You have a make or break presentation to the board. How will you cope?

- You have to dive from a ten-metre board in front of millions of television viewers. This dive will determine if you fulfil your lifetime ambition and win an Olympic medal. No second chances. How will you cope?

By their nature, you cannot predict when or why crises will emerge, nor do you know what they will be about. But you can be sure that there will be a crisis. The good news is that if you prepare properly, you can handle any moment of truth better.

Cultivate the habit of choice

In any moment of truth, there are four steps to taking control and making the most of the moment:

- Slow down internally: gain control of your emotions and impulses.
- Slow down external events: buy time and create space to find a smart way forward.
- Create options: avoid getting stuck in a binary win–lose and find creative solutions.
- Drive to action: take accountability.

Slow down internally: gain control of your emotions and impulses

Our impulses as humans have evolved to help us survive. Impulses are good if you want to avoid being eaten alive. Three salient characteristics of our impulses are:

- We are always predicting outcomes.
- We tend to predict negative, not positive outcomes.
- Our response to threat is fight, flight or freeze.

We are always predicting outcomes. Arguably, we should be called homo prospectus, not homo sapiens, because we have evolved always to be predicting. As a test, try reading the passage below:

> Cadgmbrie Unvtirseiy fnuod taht rederars mkae snsee of snetecnes wcihh are wtiretn wtih jmedblud up wrods buacsee we raed wlohe

> wdors not iudnvdiial lteters. We pcrdiet the mnniaeg of ecah wrod from the fsrit and lsat lteter of ecah wrod. Hmauns lkie to pcerdit.
>
> My porof rdaeer wlil go czray pfoornig tish, and selpl ckecher htaes tish too.

It may not be the easiest text to read. Typically, there will be an 11% cost in terms of increased effort required to read the text.[121] We are always seeking meaning, even in the nonsense above, and we are always predicting. This is why most people find the 'halfalogue' conversation so annoying: when you hear someone talking on the phone, you are hearing a halfalogue, not a dialogue and it is hard to stop your brain from wanting to complete the other half of the dialogue.

We tend to predict negative, not positive outcomes. The rustling in the bushes might be a friend or a foe: if you always assume it is a friend, you will be eaten by a lion or robbed by a mugger eventually. Negativity bias is survival bias.

Negativity bias influences how we make decisions. Let's assume someone makes you an offer. You can play a game of toss the coin where there is one toss and one toss only. If you guess correctly, you win £1,000. How much would you pay to play this game? Rationally, you should be prepared to pay up to £500, provided you are confident that the toss will be fair. Typically, most people will refuse to pay more than £350–£400 to take part: the fear of loss far outweighs the prospect of gain in this game.

Our response to threat is fight, flight or freeze. This is inevitable when we predict a negative outcome as a result of the two above. All our energy goes into our body and we focus on survival. This is good for action, bad for thinking. We stop thinking about alternatives: we just run for our lives. This helps in the bush, not in the boardroom. Fleeing or freezing in the boardroom will not help you. Fighting is often counter-productive anywhere in the firm. Descending into the "I said she said he didn't you meant and they should have ..." discussion gets you nowhere fast.

At this point, the challenge is to regain control of your emotions and impulses. If you can do this, you are well on the way to success.

The Stanford Marshmallow test[122]

16 children were, separately, offered the chance to have a marshmallow now, or two if they could wait for a few minutes. That is a devious and cruel choice to put in front of a four-year-old. Some gobbled up the marshmallow immediately, some tried to hold out for the second reward but failed. A few showed heroic self-discipline and got their second marshmallow.

The real test started over the following decades, when the researchers followed up on the children. They found that the children who showed better impulse control went on to achieve higher SAT scores, better educational outcomes and they even had a lower body mass index (BMI).[123] The second marshmallow was not a matter of greed, but of self-discipline and impulse control.

The test and the results have been replicated many times since. MRI scans show that the high-impulse control group had significant differences in their prefrontal cortex and ventral striatum: their brains operated differently.[124]

We face our own versions of the marshmallow test every day, where there is a temptation to respond immediately to an event or a person we fear or dislike. Reacting the wrong way under pressure can be a career-limiting move. It pays to be able to control your reactions. The first step is to slow down enough that you can make a rational choice about how you want to react, rather than relying on instinct and emotion in the moment.

I have talked to hundreds of managers about this challenge. Every effective manager has a mental trick for helping them in that sudden moment, where the mask of leadership is in danger of slipping. Here are some of the techniques I have been told:

- I count to three, just like my granny told me to.
- I breathe in deeply, just like I learned in meditation.
- I think about what my role model would do (do not use this if your role model is a mixture of Darth Vader and Vlad the Impaler).

- I become a fly on the wall and I watch what is happening with detachment, then I can decide what outcome I really want.
- I go to my happy place (in my imagination) where I always relax and feel calm.
- I imagine the other person wearing a pink tutu, then I can't get angry with them.

Each technique is different, and that is the point. It does not matter what technique you have, as long as you have some mental trick that allows you to calm down and stay in control of your emotions. Often, the critical moment might last only two or three seconds. Once you are through that, you can put your mask of leadership back on and regain control of your thoughts and emotions. You give yourself the chance of making better choices.

"The most powerful technique you can acquire to deal with moments of crisis and chaos is breathing."

Exercise 31: breathe to take control and focus

Perhaps the most powerful technique you can acquire to deal with moments of crisis and chaos is breathing. The New Zealand Defence Force[125] estimate that in a moment of crisis, such as a ship sinking, 85% of people will panic or make irrational decisions. Just by staying calm, you are ahead of 85% of your colleagues in a crisis. The result is that the New Zealand Defence Force, and the New Zealand All Black rugby champions, and US Special Forces now all teach breathing techniques as a way of staying calm and focused in the middle of chaos. It can make the difference between life and death.

In a crisis your breath is likely to be rapid and shallow, which is consistent with a fight or flight reflex. That is unhelpful in an office, where you need a calm reaction. Fortunately, you do not need to become a Buddhist monk[126] or seek enlightenment to learn to breathe well. Here is a simple exercise to learn and repeat:

- Inhale deeply for four seconds through your nose: feel your diaphragm expand, feel the cool air coming in.
- Hold for four seconds.
- Exhale slowly for four seconds through your nose, feel the warm air going out.
- Hold for four seconds.
- Repeat for three to five minutes a day for a month.

This is not an exercise to undertake when the crisis hits you: it is about preparing you for that moment. Breathing exercises are the mental equivalent of soldiers doing bench presses. The intention is not that soldiers should start doing bench presses when the enemy attack, but the bench presses help them give them strength when they need it. Breathing exercises are the same: they give you the ability to stay calm and focused when you need it.

Breathing and the other tricks above help you when faced with an unplanned moment of high stress. But you will often find yourself facing moments of planned high stress: the big sales pitch, the big presentation, the final interview for your dream job. For these high stress events, you need another approach. You need to find a way of staying cool, calm and collected both before and during the event. You have to get into the zone and stay there for as long as it takes.

Fortunately, there is a proven way of dealing with these moments of planned stress. You have three tools at your disposal:

- mastery
- preparation
- visualisation.

Mastery builds confidence. If you know you are expert in your topic, you will feel far more confident about that big presentation than if you are presenting on the subject for the first time to a group of experts. Concert pianists may feel nervous before a concert, but mastery is what gives them the confidence to perform. It may take years of practice to achieve true mastery. But even a limited amount of practice will enable you to overcome your worst fears, especially if you are able to practise in the same place where the event will take place. Familiarity reduces the fear of the unknown.

Preparation is vital for any high-stakes event. The best salesperson I ever met only did about three formal calls per week, which appears to be very idle. But he prepared for each one in detail and, as a result, each call would turn into a knockout meeting for a high-value sale. Spies report[127] that much of their time is spent waiting and preparing in hotel rooms. Preparing a conversation is much harder than preparing a presentation: you are in control of a presentation and the flow is set. A conversation could go in many different ways, and you have to prepare for every outcome.

"Preparing a conversation is much harder than preparing a presentation."

Visualisation is now a standard technique of sportspeople facing high-stakes events. Visualisation is a way of helping you cope mentally with a big moment by making it seem both familiar and routine. It is a powerful exercise to deploy in advance of high stakes events where you need to be at your very best.

Exercise 32: visualise to prepare for success

When you visualise, you need to experience the whole event in your mind in as much vivid detail as possible, using all your senses:

- What will it look like and what will you see? What will the lights be like?
- What sounds will you hear? Who will be speaking and what might they say?
- What will you smell?
- How will you feel, what will the temperature be like?
- How will you move and what will you do? If this is a presentation, imagine getting on stage, using the clicker to advance the slides. Imagine and rehearse every little detail.

As you visualise yourself succeeding, you should also visualise yourself overcoming obstacles successfully. Be prepared for success in any scenario. By the time you start your high-stakes event, it should no longer feel unfamiliar and threatening. It should be like a familiar movie in which you are the hero (or heroine) who succeeds. You should then be ready to act your part.

For instance, the first time I was asked to present to the board of a big firm, I was terrified by the prospect. So I made an unusual request: I asked to use the boardroom a couple of times before my big day. Because the boardroom was meant just for the board, it was rarely used, so I was given access. I rehearsed my presentation there and become thoroughly familiar with the setting and the logistics of how things worked. I even rehearsed sitting outside the room and waiting. And I invited some colleagues for a meeting there, so I could experience what it was like to be locked in debate in such a grand place. When it was time for my presentation, I no longer felt that I was entering unknown and hostile territory. Instead, I experienced familiar conditions that left me relatively calm and confident.

Portraits of resilience: impulse control and visualisation

Leon Taylor, Olympic diving medallist

High board diving is high stakes. Unlike the long jump, you only get one chance. "It is gladiatorial," says Leon, "it screws your head. If you are too laid back, it is no good. If you are too nervous, it is no good."

Twenty years of training from the age of six helped Leon to arrive at the top of the diving board at the Athens Olympics. But all that training would count for nothing if he could not cope with the intense pressure of the biggest event, biggest audience and biggest moment of his career. This was not Leon's 1% moment, it was his 0.00001% moment. He was going to be a hero or a zero as a result of a two-second dive. No second chance, no retakes.

How would you cope?

A vital part of his training was visualisation. As he talked about it,[128] he was taking himself back to Athens. "One of the most powerful tools we worked on tirelessly was visualisation. The unconscious cannot tell the difference between what is imagined and what is real. So you can prepare yourself for the future, for an event you have never been at. So I would visualise myself doing my dive to the best of my ability, in the setting you are going to do it in. I can still do it."

Leon then closed his eyes and started visualising the dive: it was clear he was mentally back at the Olympics: "I am on the end of the diving board in Athens. I can hear the murmur of 16,000 people, mainly to the right of me. I can see the water there. I can feel my feet gripping the board beneath me. I can hear that funny sound the water makes and a big crowd makes. I can also feel the electric atmosphere. I can smell the chlorine. I can even smell Pete (his diving partner) over there: he smells of chlorine too. I can feel my breathing slowing down. And then I am in the zone and I can do the dive."

Note that his visualisation encompassed all the senses he would encounter: sight, sound, smell, touch and even the feeling of his breathing and his feet. He completely immersed himself in visualising the perfect dive before the event, so that when he got to the event he was in a familiar place executing a familiar routine.

But behind 2 seconds of excellence stood 20 years of training that required huge resilience. His training regime was a 20-year growth programme (Chapter 9), constantly pushing and refining boundaries of performance. Excellence was helped by being part of a high-performance culture (Chapter 10) at Sheffield University. He had a high sense of mutual accountability with his diving partner: both kept each other honest in performance. He had a clear sense of mission (Chapter 8), having decided at the age of six that he wanted to perform in the Olympics. He learned to put emotions to work (Chapter 2) so that when competitors, or more often their parents, tried to upset him, he would use the resulting anger to spur him on. As with all top performers, he put in huge sacrifice: "I missed weddings, funerals, Christmas and fell out with friends." But he did it because he was committed to his mission and he enjoyed it.

Slow down external events: buy time and create space to find a smart way forward

In a crisis, events can move very fast. It is easy for instincts and impulse to take over. This can be useful. If you are crossing a road and you see that a car is about to hit you, you do not want to sit in the middle of the road and start a brainstorming session to find the optimum response to the car. You need to get out of the way fast, and your instincts will serve you very well.

In business, most crises do not happen in milliseconds. They unfold over minutes, hours and days. Despite this, it is easy to see colleagues succumbing to impulse and going into fight, flight or freeze mode:

- Fight: start blaming everyone else.
- Flight: start displacement activity, such as long analyses and reports which give the appearance of doing something but achieve nothing.
- Freeze: keep a low profile and hope that the crisis goes away or that someone else deals with it.

These are not helpful reactions.

Slowing things down in a business crisis achieves two goals. First, it lets you take the emotional heat out of a crisis. Second, it helps you understand what is actually going on. It lets reason displace emotion, which is a good start.

> "Take the emotional heat out of a crisis."

Exercise 33: slow down external events

In the heat of the moment, the easiest way to buy time is to ask questions, in particular open questions. This lets your colleagues blow off steam and lets you find out what is really going on. Open questions are ones to which a yes or no answer is not possible:

- Why do you say that?
- What else do you know about this?
- How did the other person react?
- What does our customer/boss/colleague think about this?

If you cannot think of a good open question, then "Say more" is a favourite: it is totally neutral and encourages them to keep talking while you keep thinking. At this point, do not offer judgements, because that is dangerous. Fighting crises with criticism is like fighting fire with gas: entertaining but not advisable. Judgements lead to arguments.

Once they start to calm down, you can move to a second technique: paraphrasing. Say back to the speaker what you heard them say, in your own words. This is powerful. It slows things down and it shows that they have been listened to and understood: it shows that their fears have been recognised. If there is any misunderstanding, you will quickly hear about this and you will be able to act on it. Once you have calmed the situation down for yourself and your colleagues, you can move to the next step: creating some options.

> "Fighting crises with criticism is like fighting fire with gas: entertaining but not advisable."

Create options: avoid getting stuck in a binary win–lose and find creative solutions

We always have choices, even if they are uncomfortable choices. If you work in a job you dislike, then every day you go into work you make a choice to continue doing something you dislike. It may not be an active choice, but it is still a choice you are making by default.

The point of slowing down is to give yourself enough time and space to make a purposeful choice, instead of defaulting to an automatic response. Even if you are caught below decks on a sinking ship, you still have choices, if you are aware of them.

"We always have choices, even if they are uncomfortable choices."

Creative choices in extreme circumstances

In September 2018, the MV Nyerere was crossing Lake Victoria towards Ukara island.[129] It had capacity for 100 people, but was carrying many more than that after a busy market day. As the passengers moved to one side to get a better view, the ship capsized and over 200 people died in the tragedy.

Being below decks is not a good place to be when a ship capsizes. Alphonce Chaharani was the ship's engineer and he was in the engine room. What options do you have in such bleak circumstances? Water was coming in everywhere, and doorways and gangways were blocked with people struggling to get out.

Alphonce did not panic and did not join the crowds rushing to get off the stricken ship. He calmly picked up some keys, and went and locked himself in a small room beneath decks. This was not a suicide act: it was a survival act. Two days later, rescuers heard a tapping sound from beneath the upturned ship's hull. It was Alphonce, who had managed to find and create an air pocket in which he could survive long enough to be rescued.

Even in an emergency, slowing down to not panic can help you identify choices which might just save your life.

Exercise 34: find creative options

There are two effective ways of creating options and choices in even the most difficult situations: seek help and be prepared.

- **Seek help.** You will find a better solution as a team than you will alone. A classic team-building exercise is desert survival or space survival.[130] The exercise gives you a list of about 20 survival items, and you have to pick the five you would take with you in an emergency. You then repeat the exercise as a group. Invariably, the group solution turns out to be better than the best individual solution, even when there is an expert in the group.
- **Be prepared.** Always have a Plan B. Many setbacks are fairly predictable. Knowing your options in advance allows you to deal with the setback if it arrives. It also gives you much more confidence in pursuing Plan A, which makes it less likely you will have to call on Plan B.

Whatever your situation, have a Plan B:

- If the negotiations do not go as you want, what is your Plan B?
- If your current job or boss is no good, what is your Plan B?
- If a supplier or colleague lets you down, what is your Plan B?
- If you do not get the raise, promotion or project you want, what is your Plan B?

Having a Plan B insures you against adversity and gives you control. Take a moment to review some of the predictable challenges you are going to be facing: what is your Plan B for all of them?

> "Always have a Plan B."

Always have a Plan B

I was in the deep Arctic in late winter on a research trip with a Saami reindeer herder, Lars Matthis. The ice gave way and my leg went through. This is not good.

> Arctic boots have several layers. On the inside, you wear a felt boot for warmth. On the outside, you wear a plastic boot to keep the damp out. Unfortunately, a plastic boot also keeps the water in, once you have gone into the freezing water. A wet boot soon becomes a frozen boot and frozen foot: end of foot.
>
> We were a day or so away from the nearest help. What would you do?
>
> Lars immediately pulled some dry summer grass out of his pack and fashioned a dry inner boot out of the grass in place of the felt. After a few changes, everything was dry again and the crisis did not turn into a disaster. In summer, Lars had prepared his Plan B for winter, and I kept my foot as a result.

Drive to action: take accountability

Crises are those moments of truth where leaders step up and followers step back. They are your chance to shine and to accelerate your career: you succeed fast or you fail fast.

> **"Leaders step up and followers step back."**

If you wish to survive, the smart thing to do is to avoid any risk: step back and let someone else step up. You may survive, but that is a weak form of resilience. You are relying on the goodwill of strangers, colleagues or even rivals for your survival. Strong-form resilience is about thriving in adversity and being able to take control of your destiny. The good news is that the more you practise stepping up, the easier and more natural it becomes. The more you practise stepping back, the more that becomes natural and the less able you are to step up when you really need to.

Exercise 35: handle a crisis

So how do you handle a crisis for success? Here are five things you should do:

- **Step up.** Do not run away from the crisis: run into it, and take ownership of it. This is the moment where no one is sure what to do, everyone is afraid of messing up. There is a leadership vacuum and it is there for you to fill. So fill it, which can be as easy as suggesting a solution and being ready to take it forwards.
- **Get help.** Lone heroes succeed in movies, not in real life. Leadership is a team sport. So get advice, get help, get resources, get backing from power brokers. Build your coalition. Don't waste time trying to persuade the doom mongers: focus on the willing and the able who can help you.
- **Drive to action, any action.** Analysis is easy and useless. Action is hard and risky. But people need to be jolted out of inactivity. The first step might be very small, like making some phone calls. It might even be the wrong first step: that does not matter because once you have momentum, you can always change direction if you need.
- **Act the part.** Long after the crisis is over, no one will remember exactly what you did, but they will remember what you were like. Learn to wear the mask of leadership: project confidence, hope, clarity and certainty because that is what people crave in a crisis.
- **Share the credit.** When it is over, be generous in giving away all the credit. By doing so, everyone will love you and the power brokers will recognise that you must have been the person driving it, if you are the one who is able to allocate all the credit. You gain credit by giving it away.

Do those five things and you turn their crisis into your opportunity.

Summary

To build lasting resilience, you cannot become a victim of external events or internal impulses. There are occasional moments of truth that will define your future. These are the times you need to be able to control your internal impulses, control external events and take responsibility for your destiny. Follow four steps to make the most of any planned, or unplanned, moment of truth in your life:

Slow down internally: gain control of your emotions and impulses

For unplanned moments of truth, do enough to stop your impulses taking over. It does not matter what mental trick you have, as long as you have one that works for you. It can be anything from counting to three to imagining the other person in a pink tutu. Do what it takes to avoid an emotional and impulsive response you may regret later.

For planned moments of truth, there are three well-established tools:

- Mastery: the more skilled you are, the easier it is do deal with difficult situations.
- Preparation: time spent in preparation is rarely wasted.
- Visualisation: visualise success in rich detail and in context. This makes the unfamiliar familiar and allows you to perform at your best.

Slow down external events: buy time and create space to find a smart way forward

Slow down your colleagues so that they do not succumb to impulses. Let them talk. Ask open questions. Recognise their fears by paraphrasing them appropriately. Only when they have calmed down, can they act rationally.

Create options: avoid getting stuck in a binary win–lose and find creative solutions

Ask for help. A collective solution beats an individual solution nearly every time because it will be better and there will be more support for making it happen. Always have a Plan B. This gives you more confidence in pursuing Plan A and makes it less likely that you have to call on Plan B.

Drive to action: take accountability

You always have choices, even if they are uncomfortable choices. Step up and take control: do not let others dictate your fate for you.

Chapter
8

Craft your mission: the power of purpose

The greatest acts of sustained resilience and sacrifice have been sustained by individuals with a very strong sense of purpose. Top athletes, great explorers and freedom fighters all have a clear purpose that drives them to extreme effort. Finding purpose in bookkeeping is harder than finding purpose in climbing Everest.

If your job does not give you meaning, you have to give meaning to your job. That is the art of job crafting, which is the focus of this chapter. The four keys to this act of job crafting are:

- Build your sense of purpose.
- Achieve mastery in what you do.
- Find autonomy.
- Build trusted relationships at work.

> "If your job does not give you meaning, you have to give meaning to your job."

Why it matters

Perhaps you imagine retiring gracefully at the age of 60, 65 or even 70. That is not how Hokusai, Japan's most famous artist, thought. He produced perhaps the best-known image of Japanese art: the *Great Wave* which now adorns mugs, posters and tea towels around the world. It shows a foaming blue claw of a wave overwhelming some boats and even overwhelming Mount Fuji in the background. It was revolutionary in its time: it was Impressionist before the Impressionists were born, and it deeply influenced them.

Hokusai was aged 70 when he produced the *Great Wave*. Although he had been learning his craft for over 50 years, this was not the apex of his career, it was the start:

> All I have done before the age of 70 is not worth bothering with. At 75, I'll have learned something of the pattern of nature, of animals, of plants, of trees, birds, fish and insects. When I am 80, you will see real progress. At 90, I shall have cut my way deeply into the mystery of life itself. At 100 I shall be a marvellous artist. At 110, everything I create – a dot, a line – will jump to life as never before.[131]

Hokusai had a burning passion to master art. His final words were to ask for a few more years to paint. His deathbed regret was, in effect, that he had not spent enough time in the office. He asked that the name on his gravestone be 'Gakyo Rojin Manji' – Old Man Mad about Painting. Not many of us will want a tombstone declaring 'Old Woman Mad about Bookkeeping' or the equivalent.

Purpose and passion are the hallmarks of people who show great resilience in the face of adversity, and who sustain high performance. Top athletes endure endless hours of hard training in pursuit of their goal, and adventurers put everything on the line to circumnavigate the world, cross Antarctica or explore the deserts and jungles of our world. But it is far easier to have purpose and passion when pursuing a personal goal. It is easier to be passionate about becoming a great painter than it is to be passionate about becoming a great bookkeeper.

"Purpose and passion are the hallmarks of people who show great resilience in the face of adversity."

The challenge in the workplace is about purpose and passion, motivation and commitment. Firms like to demand passion. Coca-Cola, Genentech, Adidas, Kellogg's, P&G, Southwest Airlines and many more have passion as one of their core firm-wide principles.[132]

Clearly, passion is far better than apathy. But you cannot order people to be passionate about soft drinks, cereal or cleaning products. It is like telling them to be happy.

Although firms demand passion, they often discourage it. The twentieth-century firm was based on scalable efficiency and predictable processes with stable rhythms and routines. This was highly efficient and effective. But it turned staff into cogs in the machine. Humans ceased to be people when they became resources to be managed by human resources: too often, humanity lost to the resources in HR.

"You cannot order people to be passionate."

You can find endless books and theories on how to motivate other people. Many of them are good. But the resilience challenge is to find what sustains your motivation for the 40 or 50 years of your career. If you rely on being motivated by your boss or firm, you are no longer in control of your destiny. You are also likely to be disappointed. Although 68% of managers rate themselves good at motivation, only 32% of their team members agree.[133] Don't expect your boss to motivate you: motivation comes from you, not your boss or your firm.

"Motivation comes from you, not your boss or your firm."

Personal motivation comes in two flavours: extrinsic and intrinsic. We will sample each flavour and see how they taste. Take a look at the list below and see what motivates you the most.

Extrinsic motivators	**Intrinsic motivators**
Money, cars, houses	Close relationships
Promotion	Personal growth, experiences
Fame	Health and fitness
Popularity	Autonomy, freedom, choice

The chances are that all of these motivate you to some extent. What motivates you at work may differ from what motivates you at home.

Extrinsic motivation is about pleasure and pain, or carrots and sticks. The rewards you might promise yourself include having great holidays, eating good food, buying a big house and a prestigious car. The prospect of all these pleasures is one way of finding the commitment to work hard. Company pay and reward schemes push you to achieve more in return for fulfilling these life dreams.

But this sort of extrinsic motivation is an accelerating treadmill to nowhere. However fast you run, you will never catch your dream because your dream is always growing faster than you can run. This is the problem of the 'hedonic treadmill'. There is always a better house, car or holiday you can buy. Worse, there is always someone you know who has a better house, car or holiday. The hedonic treadmill is a race you can never win. You will never have enough money and goods to change your level of happiness and satisfaction.

"Extrinsic motivation is an accelerating treadmill to nowhere."

Extrinsic motivation can also be a source of demotivation. For instance, investment banks are full of talented and very driven people. They work in a money machine: they are driven to make money for the bank and for themselves. It is also a highly competitive environment, where self-worth becomes defined by net worth. Money, success and self-esteem are all closely wrapped up together. Performance is closely monitored. At one bank, an annual appraisal score of 9.8 out of 10 is regarded as average, 9.7 is survivable and 9.5 out of 10 is a message that your time is over. But what really matters is how this translates into money.

I was astonished to find one client in a fury after receiving a $250,000 bonus. He was raging and ranting. The $250,000 was not going to change his life, or even his year: it was not that important. What mattered was some of his peers earned bigger bonuses.

Money had become a source of humiliation to him, and was evidence to him that he had been cheated. Money can motivate, but it also demotivates.

Social media has created a new hedonic treadmill for us, where we seek endless likes and affirmations from friends and strangers. Sean Parker, founding President of Facebook, made it clear that their goal was to "consume as much of your time and conscious attention as possible". The method was simple: "We need to sort of give you a little dopamine hit every once in a while, because someone liked or commented on a photo or a post or whatever. And that's going to get you to contribute more content, and that's going to get you ... more likes and comments. It's a social-validation feedback loop ... exactly the kind of thing that a hacker like myself would come up with, because you're exploiting a vulnerability in human psychology."[134] He was designing an addiction machine, and, as with all addictions, the short-term hit simply leads to the need for more. And the brain always craves more dopamine.

"Money can motivate, but it also demotivates."

The evidence shows that extrinsic motivators, and demotivators, have a very short shelf-life: you get the bonus, bank the cheque and the moment is gone. A classic study looked at what happened to people who won the lottery or became paralysed. There was, inevitably, a short-term spike up or down in life satisfaction for both groups. And then came the surprise. Within a year, the lottery winners were back to where they started in terms of life satisfaction, and the paraplegics also expected to recover to the level of mental wellbeing they had previously.[135] Similar studies have shown recovery after divorce, losing a spouse, birth of a child, and females losing their job.[136] Males losing their job do suffer a long-term hit to wellbeing: their identity and meaning is more closely wrapped up in their work.

It appears that wellbeing and motivation is driven by internal factors, not external. You cannot rely on pay, good fortune, social media likes and pursuit of material wealth to sustain you in the long term. You will be like a donkey chasing the carrot dangled in front of your nose: however fast you run you will never catch your goal. You have to look inwards to sustain your journey. The good news is that your inward journey is not just cheaper, it is under your control.

> **"Wellbeing and motivation is driven by internal factors, not external."**

The hedonic slaves

The consulting firm needed hard-working, loyal and experienced staff. So it started recruiting engineers who were earning around £60,000 a year. After six weeks' training, they were then hired out to clients at £300,000 a year and given a salary of £100,000 a year. Everyone, except possibly the client, was happy.

Quickly, the engineers and their families adjusted to their new income levels.

Slowly, the firm increased their demands of the engineers and even more slowly increased their salaries. They found themselves working harder, with more anti-social hours. Questionable ethical demands started emerging. The engineers kept quiet and kept working. They knew that they could not get higher pay elsewhere. They also knew that their families would struggle to adjust back to their old income levels. They were stuck, and their employer knew it.

Adjusting lifestyle upwards is easier than adjusting down. Once you are hooked on the champagne and caviar lifestyle, it is hard to go back to the beer and burgers lifestyle. At that point, you do not find freedom: you find you are a slave to your pay cheque.

The battle between extrinsic and intrinsic motivation is not new. Greek philosopher Aristotle wrote nearly 2,500 years ago:

> Happiness belongs more to those who have cultivated their character and mind to the uttermost, and kept acquisition of external goods within moderate limits, than it does to those who have managed to

> acquire more external goods than they can possibly use, and are lacking goods of the soul ... Any excessive amount of such things must either cause its possessor some injury, or, at any rate, bring him no benefit.[137]

Science is slowly catching up with what has long been known, and often been forgotten. Research is now consistently showing that chasing extrinsic goals leads to lower life satisfaction, and is less sustainable in the long term, than chasing intrinsic goals.[138] It is time to follow Aristotle and see if we can acquire some 'goods of the soul'.

Cultivate the habit: the four pillars of intrinsic motivation at work

The other flavour of motivation is intrinsic. This is where you do something because you enjoy it. The ideas of work and enjoyment rarely sit closely together. But we have seen that when they do come together, as with Hokusai, then resilience is a natural outcome: you keep going because you want to keep going.

Firms go to great lengths to work out how to motivate staff. Inevitably, the desire to motivate meets the desire to save money. The finance department usually wins. Pay and benefits are sliced and diced in a thousand creative ways to make as little go as far as possible. Offices are redesigned to be funky, but more and more hot desks get crammed in. Flexible working hours are encouraged, but somehow flexibility turns into being flexibly on call 24/7. More motivation with less money is a never-ending challenge.

If you rely on your firm for your motivation, you will be disappointed. Even firms that work hard to provide the funkiest and latest in employee engagement struggle. Average tenure at Google is just over a year, while eBay, Qualcomm and Apple all have average employee tenure of around two years.[139] This puts them in the bottom decile for Fortune 500 firms.

Relying on your firm for your motivation and commitment is victim mentality: you are letting your state of mind be determined by other people who may or may not have your best interests at heart. To sustain motivation for 40 or 50 years, your motivation has to come from within.

The four pillars of intrinsic motivation at work are:[140]

- purpose: craft your job to find meaning and purpose
- mastery
- relationships
- autonomy.

You can use these four pillars to support your own growth, and you can also use them to support your team members.

Constructing these pillars well is job crafting.[141] You take your existing role, strip it down to its essentials and then rebuild it so that it more clearly fits what you want and need. This involves both reality and perception. You can probably reshape or refocus your role to some extent, but you can also think about what you do in a different way. By shifting both reality and perception, you can dramatically change your engagement with your role. Increased engagement is the gateway to higher performance; higher performance and higher engagement sustain resilience.

Cultivate the habit: craft your job to find meaning and purpose

We have already seen that a strong sense of purpose can drive people to sustain extraordinary efforts over a long time. Hokusai kept on working until his death, aged 89. In 2019, it was still possible to see Herbert Blomstedt conducting major orchestras around the world. He was slow-moving on stage, but at the age of 92 you are entitled to slow down slightly. Once on the podium, he burst into life and showed total enthusiasm and pleasure in a calling he has pursued for over 60 years.

At 75, Mick Jagger is still prancing around the world with the Rolling Stones, singing "This may be the last time", and hoping that it won't be the last time. But how can you have a sense of purpose and passion if you are working in the middle of an organisation that makes snacks or provides accounting services, or you are cleaning toilets all day?

There is an old and much told story of the three stonemasons in the distant past. When asked what they were doing, they all gave different replies:

- "I hack at stones all day."
- "I am using my craft to build a building."
- "I am working for the glory of god and building a cathedral: my craft and skill will be admired long after I am gone."

"Can you convert your job or career into a calling?"

700 years ago, there were no psychologists on hand to measure the resilience and motivation of each of the three stonemasons. You can decide for yourself which of them was going to be the most committed. They were all doing the same job, but they saw it in completely different ways. The first was doing a job, the second had a career and the third had a calling. They provide a simple example of job crafting by creating purpose and meaning from your work. Are you hacking stones all day or building a legacy that will be admired? Can you convert your job or career into a calling?

The power of purpose

Having a real sense of purpose might save your life. Victor Frankl was a neurologist and psychologist who landed up in concentration camps during World War II. He survived and the experience shaped his views. He observed that those inmates who had a sense of purpose and meaning were more likely to survive than those without. In his words: "Everything can be taken from a man but one thing: the last of the human freedoms – to choose one's attitude in any given set of circumstances, to choose one's own way."[142]

Even in the most extreme circumstances, we still have some choice over how we choose to react.

Amy Wrzesniewski, a professor at University of Michigan, decided to find out whether staff saw themselves as having a job, a career or a calling.[143] Being an academic, she researched the material available to her: staff working at her institution and the institutions of her colleagues. The first, and unsurprising, finding was that higher-status staff were more likely to see themselves as having a calling. If you are a professor, it is easy to see that you have a calling. So she dug a little deeper and explored a lower status group: administrators. To her surprise, she found that even this group split roughly evenly between those who thought they had a job, a career or a calling. You can see and experience the same work in profoundly different ways.

To see how you can turn any job into a calling, we will visit Jason who was a janitor at Providence St Vincent Medical Centre. Janitors are at the bottom of the food chain when it comes to status. Surgeons are like gods, nurses are like angels and janitors are like wallpaper: ideally, you never even notice them. The hours are often anti-social because hospitals are 24/7 operations and the pay is low. Low pay, tough hours and low status is pretty thin gruel for an exercise in job crafting.

But Jason saw that his job was not just about wielding a mop and clearing up. He saw the patients were often anxious and many were lonely because they had few visitors. He learned to size up patients as he did his work. Some wanted to be alone with their thoughts, others wanted to talk to someone, and others just wanted the comfort of a smile. He started to engage with patients, and they started to engage with him. He started to receive compliments as patients noticed his smile brought a ray of sunshine into their day.

Like the medieval bricklayers, Jason was redefining his job. He was no longer just mopping floors, he was helping patients. He was transforming himself from cleaner to healer. In doing so, he not only found purpose: he also got the support of patients who were happy to see him.

Jason was not alone. All the support staff at the hospital came together to produce a wild and brilliant 'pink glove dance' to raise awareness of breast cancer. The dance is available online and is a good way to waste (or invest) four minutes of your time at work.[144]

A good way to start your job crafting is to look beyond your immediate tasks. If you had to describe your work to a five-year-old, you would probably have to say something like, "I spend my time talking to people, writing emails and working on a computer." This task list is understandable, but not inspirational. In truth, even the most glamorous jobs have their fair share of dull and routine work.

> **"Even the most glamorous jobs have their fair share of dull and routine work."**

Even at senior levels, I meet clients who are fed up with routine. One leading libel lawyer was apparently highly successful and wealthy. His focus and specialisation over many years brought both success and boredom: "Every case is basically the same: I wish I could do something different instead of dealing with all these big and fragile egos every day." More simply, a senior marketing executive wailed: "I have been doing on-pack coupons for 25 years. I never want to see another on-pack coupon again in my life!" From the outside, these people seem to embody success and glamour, but from the inside, they think their work is dull and boring.

Top purpose

It was a huge reception in Jakarta. Some people love these opportunities to network, I dread the prospect of having to make small talk to strangers. As I mingled, I bumped into someone whom nobody was approaching. So I introduced myself and asked what he did.

"My job is to increase the prosperity of the nation," he replied. What sort of job is that, I asked myself.

> Closer enquiry revealed that he was the Governor of the Central Bank, Bank Indonesia. That is a role that is highly technical and detailed, but also highly political with high public scrutiny. It is high pressure and requires high resilience. But the way he thought of his job gave him clear purpose and meaning: this came through in the energy and vigour he brought to the job.
>
> To his credit, he forgave my bumbling introduction and we worked together successfully to help transform the bank. Finding meaning in your role makes a difference, no matter how senior or junior you may be.

Looking for meaning and purpose in your immediate tasks is like searching for smoke signals in the fog: it is an exercise in futility. Instead, start looking for purpose by understanding who you are helping and the benefits you are helping them achieve. The janitor could see this: he was helping people heal. The senior executives could not see beyond their dull daily routine.

You can find meaning in your work when you can feel and understand its ultimate purpose. For instance, fundraising by phone is hard graft: dialling for dollars. In one simple experiment, researchers found that a five-minute conversation with a beneficiary of a US university scholarship raised fundraising performance by more than 50% over two weeks, relative to fundraisers who had no conversation with the beneficiary. Fundraising was no longer just about hitting a target, it became a way of helping real people, real students.

When your boss is an algorithm, your boss is a tyrant who will squeeze the most efficiency out of every minute of your day. This is the fate of many people who work in package delivery: it is an unremitting race against time. So how can you find purpose and meaning as a delivery driver, handler or despatcher? FedEx created the famous concept of the 'golden package'. This is the package that is potentially life-saving or life-transforming to the recipient. In the words of a famous 2007 FedEx advertisement: "Come hell or high water, it must be delivered safely".[145] But, of course, the courier has no idea which package is the golden package, so every package must be treated as if it is the golden package. Perhaps not surprisingly, FedEx has the top decile employee tenure among the Fortune 500 at over six years.[146]

It pays to understand your true purpose. I talked to nurses in both the NHS and in private hospitals. The nurses in the NHS felt overwhelmed, overworked and overmanaged. They had a calling, but it was being submerged by administration and work overload. Despite this, the public service ethos is very strong and anything to do with the private sector is disliked intensely. I then asked the nurses in the private hospitals why they had abandoned the public sector, especially as there was little difference in pay. "Easy," said one nurse, "here we actually have time to look after patients instead of looking after forms. In the private sector I can be a nurse, not a form-filler."

Portraits of resilience: power of purpose

David Stephen, Head of Risk

Since the great global financial crisis, bankers have been public enemy number one, ahead even of politicians, estate agents and second-hand car dealers. So who do the bankers hate? Pretty uniformly, they all hate their risk officers. Risk officers are the spoil sports who stop bankers making dodgy deals, which will earn a huge bonus this year and cost a fortune later when the deal goes sour. How do you survive for decades in a career where your colleagues hate what you do?

David Stephen is Head of Risk[147] at RBS and recognises this challenge: "Most people in the bank want more: more profit, more deals, more of everything. I am the only one who wants less: less risk." But he sees this positively: "The West has had suppressed growth rates for ten years because of the financial crisis. This has caused huge pain and people losing jobs and houses. My job is to make sure that no bank I work for fails and contributes to that happening again. Helping to run a bank is a privilege. I see myself as the chief solutions officer for the bank. You have to stay true to values you believe in."

If your job is to say no to colleagues endlessly, you will find it hard to sustain enthusiasm for long. If you see your job as finding solutions and helping both the bank and society at large to prosper, you are more likely to sustain a long-term career. Having moral purpose sustains energy.

As with all resilient leaders, David has layers of resilience. In risk, you need resilience because it is easy to get fired for mistakes that others have made but you have not stopped. Reaching out (Chapter 5) and clear choices (Chapter 7) made all the difference early in his career when "you know you may be fired and your face will be on the front pages of the papers next morning. But if you have a strong and supportive family, that is all you need. When it happened I just thought tomorrow is the start of our next adventure." Knowing your choices matters in adversity. It even matters when you get up. In David's words: "Every morning you have a choice to get up as Mr Happy or Mr Grumpy." Choose well.

Of course, the easiest way to find your purpose and have a calling is to join an organisation that has a mission you are committed to. High alignment between personal and organisation missions is a good starting point for high performance and high resilience. This is the essence of Teach First, which is now the largest graduate recruiter in the UK, and its sister organisations in over 40 other countries, including Teach for America. At first sight, they have perhaps the least attractive recruiting proposition ever to appear on campus: work for half the salary and twice the grief you can get from a top bank or consulting firm. But the offer is not about money, it is about purpose: it is a chance not just to teach, but to change lives. It is a highly appealing proposition to some of the best and brightest graduates in the world.

> **"Having a sense of purpose will help you stay the course."**

In similar fashion, the armed forces, church and much of the public sector provide a calling and a mission. You can find purpose by joining an organisation with a purpose you like, or you can craft your own job purpose wherever you work. Either way, having a sense of purpose will help you stay the course and sustain high performance.

Finding purpose in the street[148]

Ian (now Lord) Wrigglesworth was campaigning in Stockton market in the north of England. He was a popular MP with an unpopular party, so he faced a struggle to get re-elected and save his job. Many people came up to him and thanked him for his work. He had a good word for everyone he met. Whatever job people had, Ian would find a way of exclaiming delight and admiration for the work they did. Ian understood the power of flattery.

One man came up and started thanking Ian for helping out on a problem with his business. Ian gently asked to be reminded what the business was. The man looked slightly embarrassed by the question and admitted, under his breath, that he was a pawnbroker.

This was an interesting moment: how do you express delight and admiration for a pawnbroker? Typically, they are seen as exploiting people when they are most in need. Without blinking an eyelid, Ian exclaimed "Excellent! Pawnbrokers were the original bankers. You invented banking. And to this day, you provide banking and support for those who are shunned by the big banks. Yours is a vital service!"

The pawnbroker visibly puffed up with pride as Ian spoke. One more vote in the bag, which was just as well: he eventually won the election by just 103 votes out of 60,000 (after three recounts).

Find pride in your purpose, and in everyone else's.

Exercise 36: craft your job to find meaning and purpose

Ultimately, all work benefits other people in some way. The goal of this exercise is to find out how your work benefits other people, and who those people are. Knowing that you make a difference is a spur to doing it as well as possible: it is the road to mastery, which also sustains motivation.

How does your work help others?

Cultivate the habit: autonomy

I was in Google's engineering centre in London. It was what you would expect: beautifully designed, hip and apparently laidback. Staff had high degrees of freedom about how and when they worked. It seemed like the sort of place to chill out, not the sort of place to work in. I went to the toilets. At head height in front of each urinal there was a framed A4 sheet of paper. It was a guide to how to identify and fix bugs in code. I was not qualified to understand the technical quality of the guide, but I fully understood its cultural quality. It sent a very simple message: no matter who you are, what you do or where you are, never never stop thinking about your job. The sign also set up an interesting multi-tasking challenge: failure to multitask well would have immediate and unfortunate consequences.

"With great freedom comes great responsibility."

Google's toilets sent a wider message about the emerging nature of work in the twenty-first century: you may have freedom, but with great freedom comes great responsibility. This is a sea change from the past. Previously, staff and managers were cogs in a machine. The job of a manager was to transmit orders down from the top and to transmit information back up. That was the essence of command and control, which firms inherited from military organisations. But the world has changed: information has been set free and no longer flows up and down. Managers are not custodians of information and orders: they have to be decision-makers, problem-solvers and leaders of people. They have much more autonomy than ever before, but with that autonomy comes the responsibility to take control and make things happen. Autonomy, like freedom, is not a free lunch.

"Autonomy, like freedom, is not a free lunch."

Most people want autonomy and freedom, even it means that the certainty and security of an old paternalistic world has been replaced by uncertainty and insecurity. Employers have lost their coercive power: we now have choice about where we work and what we do.

Freedom of choice is a vital part of resilience and high performance. If we do something from choice, we are more likely to sustain it over time than if we are told to do it. For instance, if you were told you have to go for a five-mile run every morning at 6am, you might object, even if you were told it is vital for your health. But if you choose to do it, because you enjoy the peace and quiet of the park and value the time to think, then you are more likely to keep going for 35 years and counting (as in my case). Choice becomes habit. When the reflective choice becomes reflexive habit, you can sustain your choice indefinitely.

Even government, which is used to enforcing decisions by regulation and rule of law, is starting to recognise the limits of coercion. The UK Government set up the Behavioural Insights Team (the Nudge Unit) in 2010 to see how it could nudge people into behaviours, which ultimately would benefit themselves and society through lower welfare bills, higher taxes and less crime. Some of the impacts it has had include:[149]

- reducing speeding offences in East Sussex by 20%
- achieving a 34% increase in acceptances by top universities of candidates from under-represented groups and schools
- encouraging over 100,000 more people to sign up as organ donors.[150]

Achieving each of these goals would be difficult through the normal channel of compulsion. The magic of the Nudge Unit has been to find ways of framing choices for citizens so that they make the desired choice of their own accord.

Autonomy and choice are the future of work at all levels. A car factory would seem to be more about automation than autonomy. Historically, the relentless pressure of the production line meant that humans were little more than slightly unreliable machines working to the pace of the line: the humans were part of the machine in a way that Charlie Chaplin depicted in *Modern Times*.

But a walk around the Land Rover factory in Solihull showed how times have changed.[151] At each work station, there were not only workers, there were also huge charts, which they maintained, detailing every aspect of performance of the work station. The crew would regularly review their own performance and see how they could improve it. This was revolution. In the past, managers managed performance and there was often a highly confrontational culture between managers and staff. By giving control to the front line, Land Rover was giving staff both autonomy and empowerment. The result was a transformation in terms of productivity, quality and culture: staff and managers now work together for common goals.[152]

The autonomy message is getting through to individual managers. When bosses were asked what they really wanted from their team members (as opposed to what they had to record on the formal evaluation system of the firm), this is what they said were their top five expectations:[153]

- reliability.
- hard work.
- proactivity.
- ambition.
- loyalty.

"The future has a habit of arriving late in some places."

This is an interesting set of expectations. Three of the expectations are highly traditional: reliability, loyalty and hard work could come straight from a nineteenth-century manager. But that same nineteenth-century manager would be aghast at the idea of workers being proactive and ambitious. Today, you probably do not want to be told what to do by your boss. That is fine, because your boss does not want to spend all day telling you what to do. The era of autonomy has truly arrived, although the future has a habit of arriving late in some places: there are still some bosses and firms stuck in the past.

The rise of autonomy at Land Rover and elsewhere is not happening because firms want to be nice to you. It is happening because it is vital to sustaining high performance. This is common sense. In which environment would you expect to sustain high performance in the long term:

- A twentieth-century workplace: command and control, do as you are told, little autonomy, freedom or responsibility.
- A twenty-first-century workplace: take control yourself, high autonomy, freedom and responsibility.

The twentieth-century model enabled people to sustain modest performance for many years. That is a very weak form of resilience: you survive rather than thrive. The twenty-first-century model encourages and enables you to sustain high performance in the long term: that is strong form resilience.

Exercise 37: achieve autonomy: context, earn and claim the right

Achieving autonomy is different from desiring it. You have three ways in which to achieve autonomy:

- Choose your context.
- Earn the right.
- Claim the right.

Choose your context. Not all firms or bosses believe in autonomy: some prefer the nineteenth-century to the twenty-first-century. Low autonomy organisations tend to be bureaucratic and process-driven: call centre staff reading from scripts being an extreme example. You may be put under pressure to hit targets, but you will not have to engage your brain too much. Understand the choice you are making, and be prepared to live with it.

Earn the right. Freedom and autonomy have to be earned before they are given. The more demanding the role, the longer it takes to earn the right. Royal Marine Commandos have to prove themselves over 15 months of training, hospital doctors will do about 10 years of training (depending on their speciality) before they are fully qualified. Whatever you do, you have to show that you have mastered your craft before you are allowed autonomy. Learning and mastery are the roads to autonomy and freedom.

Claim the right. It is not enough to work hard and well. You have to prove that you work well. And then you need to demand roles and assignments where you can practise your craft autonomously. If you wait for the world to recognise you, you are likely to have a very long wait. In the old world of paternalism, the firm would look after you, whereas in the new world of autonomy, you have to look after yourself.

"If you wait for the world to recognise you, you are likely to have a very long wait."

Cultivate the habit: develop supportive relationships

The importance of supportive relationships was discussed at length in Chapter 5. From a job-crafting perspective, the challenge is to make sure that you forge the right relationships with the right people. If you are a successful sole trader, you can do this by picking your clients: you only work with people you want to work with. Most of us are not in a position to pick and choose. We choose our colleagues the same way we choose our family: the choice is made for us.

In practice, you can influence your choice of colleagues by picking the firm you join. Just as employers are increasingly screening candidates on the basis of their values, so you should screen employers on the basis of their values. To do this, a good first step is to ignore their values statement: this is a formulaic set of words which are meant to look pretty in the annual report and give the non-executive directors something to talk about. The real values of a firm are defined by how people act when they think no one is watching them. You can find this out by talking to employees, ex-employees, suppliers and customers: do your due diligence, because your career depends on it.

"The real values of a firm are defined by how people act when they think no one is watching them."

Within the firm, you can choose your relationships by navigating towards the areas of the firm where you fit. In every firm there are 'Death Star' bosses, and everyone knows who they are. In an age of autonomy, your task is to control your destiny and make sure you avoid the 'Death Star' bosses. That means you do not wait for the HR machine to assign you to whatever gaps they need to fill. Actively seek out bosses you want to work for, and make yourself useful to them, be invisible and unavailable when the 'Death Star' boss comes hunting for more victims to pull into their death orbit.

Exercise 38: develop supportive relationships

If you want supportive relationships at work, you have to find the right context. That means:

- choosing the right firm
- choosing the right boss
- choosing the right projects.

These are difficult choices to make, because you may lack the knowledge or power to make the right choices. But, ultimately, only you can be accountable for your career.

Cultivate the habit: achieve mastery

Resilience without competence is impossible. We cannot sustain effort at something we are not capable of doing. I might like to sail around the world single-handed, but I would give up before leaving harbour as I have no idea how to rig a sail, tie a knot, read a nautical map or do anything else connected with sailing.

> **"Resilience without competence is impossible."**

People who have true mastery make the difficult look easy, whether it is a musician playing virtuoso music, or an athlete competing at the peak of their powers. The problem is that none of us starts with mastery of our chosen craft. So how can we build resilience through mastery when we start with no mastery? The answer is about making the journey rewarding in its own right. When you link learning and autonomy, you have a path to mastery.

Hokusai's life shows the power of the journey. He started life as a mirror maker, which was his father's trade. He then switched to art and printmaking, and spent over 75 years learning and refining his craft. Even on his death bed, he knew he had not achieved complete mastery. Hokusai's endless resilience came from a deep desire to learn: his journey mattered as much as his destination.

It is clear that Hokusai was passionate about learning and mastering his art, and this matters because you can only excel at what you enjoy. Enjoyment is not a nice-to-have: it is a must-have. To be excellent at anything takes time and effort. Malcom Gladwell popularised the idea that mastery takes 10,000 hours of deliberate practice, where 'deliberate' means you are constantly pushing your limits, and you are consciously learning using a coach or other structured learning.[154] The rule applies (more or less) to structured and stable activities such as sport, chess or medicine.

Management work is much more ambiguous, which makes mastery harder and deliberate, and structured practice is also much harder.[155] Learning to succeed in an unstructured world takes a huge amount of discretionary effort, where you consistently have to go above and beyond the immediate demands of your job. All professionals can sustain high effort for a while, when required. But sustaining high effort for the 75 years in which Hokusai produced an astonishing 30,000 works is only possible if you enjoy your work and enjoy your journey to mastery.

Thinking of mastery as a journey is the key to resilience. If I really wanted to sail the world single-handed, I would not jump on a boat and set off. I would have to serve an apprenticeship where I slowly built up all the skills and experience to undertake the venture. The joy would be in the learning and the process. At each stage of your learning journey you have to aim for the goldilocks zone: too much stretch and you blow up, too little stretch and

Fairy Liquid and the joy of mastery

Fairy Liquid is the leading washing up liquid in the UK. It is also a premium product: it is far more expensive than the competition, and is positioned as a superior product.

I took a keen interest in Fairy Liquid when I found myself selling it, and other detergents, in the north of Scotland. As I went from town to town, I started to notice that about half the households displayed a bottle of Fairy Liquid in the kitchen window. No competitor products were to be seen anywhere. I wondered if this might be a new Scottish tradition, to go along with wearing kilts and eating haggis.

Eventually, the mystery solved itself. Buying Fairy Liquid showed that you were house-proud: you kept your house in perfect condition. It was a sign of mastery, and that you took pleasure in keeping high standards. If you bought a cheap competing product, that sent all the wrong signals so you would hide your cheap detergent beneath the kitchen sink.

Mastery of housework means you take joy and pride in doing it well: mastery and autonomy march hand in hand. If you are a teenager who is forced to tidy up your bedroom, you have neither autonomy nor mastery, and the result is a slightly tidier bedroom and a much grumpier teenager.

Mastery and autonomy help you sustain high performance in anything, even housework.

you learn nothing. Keep stretching yourself just enough that you always learn, but never blow up.

This learning journey is covered in detail in the next chapter on growth. The important thing to note is that for your career, this is a journey that never ends. Whatever skills you master when you are 25 will be irrelevant or obsolete by the time you are 65: you have to keep on learning and growing. This growth allows you to adapt and thrive in a changing world.

Your role as a manager: build intrinsic motivation in your team

> "If you are not motivated, do not expect your team to feel motivated either."

As a manager you need intrinsic motivation: if you are not motivated, do not expect your team to feel motivated either. But you also need to help your team find their intrinsic motivation. Simply telling them to be motivated or giving inspiring and motivating speeches will not work. To do this, use the principles outlined in this section: focus on purpose, autonomy, relationships and mastery.

> "The best managers delegate nearly everything."

Exercise 39: build intrinsic motivation in your team

As a manager, you can help your team by focusing on the four pillars of intrinsic motivation:

1. **Purpose:** show that there is meaning and purpose in what your team does. The simple act of connecting your team to your customers can be a revelation.
2. **Autonomy:** professionals crave autonomy, so give it to them. Delegate as much as you can. If you ask what you can delegate,

the answer will be "not much". Instead, ask what you cannot delegate and again the answer will be "not much". The best managers delegate nearly everything. This tells your team that you trust them: most teams are very keen to show that they can live up to the trust you have given them.

3. **Relationships:** you are the most important relationship they have at work. Research[156] shows that bosses who are most highly rated by their teams do one thing very well: they show that they care for you and your career. Invest time and effort in doing this, and you have the basis of a productive relationship with each team member.
4. **Mastery:** you can help your team achieve mastery in two ways. First, delegate tasks that will stretch and challenge them. Second, when they ask for help, do not tell them what to do. Instead, coach them and help them discover the answers for themselves. Make them learn to depend on themselves, not on you and you will build autonomy and mastery.

If you have a team with a strong sense of purpose, that has supportive relationships, and each team member is trusted with high autonomy and is learning mastery with stretching tasks, the chances are that your team will show high performance and high resilience.

Summary

Extrinsic motivation such as pay and rewards, or chasing more material wealth or another dopamine hit from social media is a hedonic treadmill to nowhere. You will never get enough of what you chase.

Intrinsic motivation builds lasting resilience: this is where you want to do something for its own sake, not to chase a secondary goal such as money, power or fame. The four pillars of intrinsic motivation are purpose, autonomy, relationships and mastery:

- **Purpose:** whether you are a janitor or a central bank governor you can find a greater purpose in your work beyond the dull routine of your daily tasks. The key is to look at who benefits from your work and how they benefit. Everyone makes a difference to the world, including you.

- **Autonomy:** the old world of command and control produces compliance and a weak form of resilience where mediocre performance can be sustained. In a world of autonomy, you have more freedom, more responsibility, more choice and more uncertainty. This is a high-performance world, where you need to find the context, work, firm and colleagues to flourish. Find work that plays to your mastery strengths: build on your strengths, not your weaknesses.
- **Relationships:** finding a supportive culture and supportive relationships is vital to sustaining performance in the long term. Screen potential workplaces according to their values: understand how people behave when no one is watching.
- **Mastery:** you cannot sustain effort where you lack competence. Acquiring mastery requires a huge amount of discretionary effort sustained over time. That means we have to find something where we will enjoy the journey as much as the destination: you only excel at what you enjoy.

"You only excel at what you enjoy."

Chapter

Keep on learning: the power of growth

Growth is the mindset that will enable you to learn, adapt and flourish throughout your career. If you do not adapt, you cannot progress or even survive in a changing world.

Traditional training is of limited help. Your most powerful form of learning is from experience and observation. This chapter will show how you can turn the random walk of experience into a structured journey of discovery which meets your needs. A simple four-step model will let you learn in real time from everyday events, both positive and negative. It will let you build your personal success model, which you can keep on adapting to your changing circumstances.

Why growth matters

Walking through the City of London is like walking through history. The City is a living time machine. From one spot you can look up at a brand new skyscraper being built and look down at the foundations of the old Roman walls: you can span 2,000 years with a single glance.

In between the gleaming towers and teaming crowds are some old buildings belonging to livery companies. They were historically responsible for the training, quality and regulation of the main trades of the city. The livery companies include the Fletchers (arrow makers), Bowyers (Longbow makers), Coopers (barrel makers for beer) and the Tallow Chandlers: they made tallow candles and competed with the Wax Chandlers who made candles from wax.

These occupations have become historical curiosities, just as many of today's trades will become historical curiosities. In the last 100 years, the proportion of the labour force working on farms has fallen from 34% to 1.5% of the workforce,[157] while those working as professionals and managers has risen from 10% to 41% of the workforce. The hordes working in the fields have been replaced by hordes working in offices. There has been a similar shift from domestic service and labouring to clerical work. Entire industries that were major employers are now relatively minor employers: shipbuilding, mining and cotton mills are mere shadows of their former selves.

History tells us that the job you have at the start of your career is unlikely to exist when you finish your career, especially as careers and working lives become longer. That means that you have to keep on learning and adapting if you are to survive: personal growth is vital to career survival and success.

"The job you have at the start of your career is unlikely to exist when you finish your career."

As with history, so with the future. Oxford University estimates that nearly half of all jobs are at risk from artificial intelligence (AI) in the next 20 years.[158] Roughly the same finding could have been made at any time in the last 200 years: half of all jobs have always been at risk from technology since the dawn of the Industrial Revolution. In the past, it has been manual jobs that have been displaced. This time, it is more likely to be your job that is at risk: the promise of AI is that, increasingly, it will replace routine work of everyone from administrators to surgeons and lawyers. If you are engaged in repetitive work with predictable routines, your work is at risk.

In the unlikely event that both your industry and the jobs within it remain unchanged for the rest of your career, you will still face the challenge of change and growth if you want to flourish. If you are to have a successful career in anything anywhere, you will find your job keeps on changing as you are promoted and you take on more responsibility.

Every promotion you receive is a moment of triumph and crisis. The triumph is obvious, the crisis is hidden. Promotions are career crises because each promotion means that the rules of survival and success change. What succeeded at one level will not succeed at the next level. To grow in your career, you have to grow your capabilities.

"Every promotion you receive is a moment of triumph and crisis."

The challenge of growth is often felt hardest with your very first promotion. Your success formula as a team member, which led to promotion, leads to failure as a team boss. This is the challenge of 'the leader in the locker room'. Imagine the star sports player who is promoted to manage the team. As the team star he was making all the tackles, scoring goals and crafting passes. With his new responsibility, he doubles down on his success formula and now works twice as hard to score goals, make tackles and craft passes. He is then fired as a coach, because his job is not to be the best player on the team. His job is to find the best players, develop them, motivate them and set the direction and tactics for the team.

"If you don't adapt, you will work hard and fail fast."

Being a great player and a great manager are completely different skills. That is why few great players become great managers, and many great managers were journeyman players. The trap of the leader in the locker room is obvious in sports, but is invisible in firms where many leaders think it is their job to be the smartest person on the team and to tackle all the toughest challenges. If you don't adapt, you will work hard and fail fast.

The growth challenge of stepping up at work can be seen in the table below.[159]

The challenge of stepping up

Managing self: team member	Managing others: team leader
How do I do this?	Who can do this?
Deliver performance	Manage performance of others
Receive and act on feedback	Give feedback
Seek direction and support	Give direction and support
Take on challenges	Delegate challenges
Be positive	Be a role model for others
Work to clear goals	Manage ambiguity and change

Many new team leaders struggle with the first question in the table above: moving from "How do I do this task?" to "Who can do this task?" When it comes to delegating key tasks, many managers prefer to delegate to the one person they trust the most: themselves. This is a recipe for over-work and under-performance. Lack of trust has a corrosive effect on team morale, and it means that team members are not challenged to grow and raise their performance. Lack of trust and delegation hurts the performance of the team manager and the whole team.

Learning a new success model is, inevitably, risky and takes courage. You have to do less of what worked in the past and you have to try new ways of working. That is the growth challenge that everyone faces throughout their career: you simply have to keep on learning, adapting and growing.

The growth challenge does not end with your first promotion. The challenge never stops. Each step on your career journey requires that you grow and adapt, as the following table shows:[160]

The growth challenge across your career

Leadership level	**Managing self: new employee**	**Front-line management: managing others**	**Middle management: managing managers**	**Top management: managing a business and a P&L**
Time horizon	A day or a week	A week to a quarter	A quarter to a year	Over a year
Main task	Doing: quality, speed, craft skills, work planning	Managing: coach, motivate, performance management, delegation	Optimising: improve how things work	Integrating and changing the work of the business
Who you value	Self	Your team	Other functions	Staff support
Financial skills	N/A	Cost management	Budget management: negotiate and control	P&L management: revenue generation, cost allocation
Traps and challenges	Disenchantment: dull, boring work	Not changing your game	Not managing politics	From impostor syndrome to hubris

In a 40 to 50 year career you will start out by learning some craft skills such as accounting or analysis. The importance of being technically excellent in these skills reduces over your career, because you can hire plenty of people with fresher technical skills who are hungrier and lower cost than you are. Instead, you have to grow your people and political skills. You need people skills to manage people, and you need political skills to manage the organisation: aligning agendas, managing conflict and crises, influencing people and decisions and building networks of trust and support. You have to learn how to acquire and use power.

Finally, you need to keep on growing because you can no longer depend on your employer for your career. Average job tenure across the OECD is 6.1 years,[161] which contrasts with a likely 45-year career. Your continued employment no longer depends on your employer, it depends on your employability. A good way to test your employability is to see if you are getting any offers from rival firms. As one head of HR put it: "If rival firms do not want your services, then I don't either. I can always find someone hungrier and cheaper to do your job."[162]

"Continued employment no longer depends on your employer, it depends on your employability."

The four main reasons why growth is essential if you are to stay the course are:

- The industry you start in will probably change out of all recognition.
- The role you have today will change because of AI and technology.
- The rules of survival and success keep on changing as your career progresses.
- There are always younger, cheaper, hungrier people with fresher skills waiting to take your place. In a global world, you may be displaced by someone from a country you have never seen.

Learning and growth is the fuel of your career. If you do not learn and grow, you will have no career fuel and you will go nowhere fast. And this makes growth a vital part of resilience: you cannot survive without personal growth.

Growth is vital to your ability to stay the course, which is the long-term version of resilience. And growth is also a vital way to deal with crises and setbacks, which is short-term resilience. We will now explore growth in the context of both resilience in the long and short term.

"Learning and growth is the fuel of your career."

What growth means at work

How do you learn to be a manager?

Most managers are accidental managers. Typically, a good team player is promoted, and it is assumed that somehow they will just work out how they are meant to manage. This makes them accidents waiting to happen.

I have asked thousands of managers in groups how they have learned to lead. I let them choose two from six sources of learning. Try the exercise yourself. In practice, what are the two most valuable sources of learning to lead for you, from the following six options:

- books
- courses
- bosses (good and bad lessons)
- role models (inside and outside work)
- peers
- personal experience.

When I ask groups this question, virtually no one claims to learn from books or courses, which could be bad news for an author who delivers courses. Many learn from some form of second-hand experience such as observing bosses, peers and role models. This makes perfect sense: you see someone do something smart, and you may try to copy what they do. If you see someone blow up, you quietly make a note not to do the same thing. This is highly practical: it tells you what works in your context today. But by far the biggest source of learning for most people is personal experience: this is the learning that is most vivid and emotionally intense.

Learning from experience may make sense, but it has huge drawbacks:

- You depend on having the right experiences. If you work on a good project with a good boss, you learn good lessons fast and you can accelerate your career. If you work on a 'Death Star' project with a nightmare boss, you will find your career accelerating towards the exit ramp. This means that learning from experience is a random walk. If your career is a random walk, you will discover that career is a verb, not a noun: you will career unpredictably from triumph to disaster and back again.
- Learning from experience is very slow. Requiring leaders to have experience is a good way for older executives to keep younger talent out of power. But the legends of Silicon Valley started their journeys to fame and fortune in their twenties and Alexander the Great had conquered all of the known world by the age of 30. Age should not be a barrier to success, whether you are in your twenties or your sixties.
- Experiential learning is all about trial and error. That is painful for you, and it is painful for the teams you manage. It is also hazardous: making too many errors is a career-limiting move. Managers know this, and the result is stress. If you do not know how to do something but you know that getting it wrong is terminal for your career, then that is a recipe for knots in your stomach and sleepless nights.
- Learning from experience is highly inefficient. Setbacks offer us vivid and powerful lessons about how not to do something. This means we are normally very good at learning from failure. Learning from success is much more elusive: we tend to take success for granted, because that is how things ought to work. But, in practice, making things work is very hard. When things

work well, we should reflect on why they went well and what we can do to assure success in future. You have probably attended plenty of post-mortems that asked what went wrong. How many times have you had a team meeting to review a success where you asked what went right and why?

"Learning from experience is a random walk."

Experience is fuel for your learning and growth journey. But you need ways of accelerating and focusing the learning you achieve from experience. Books and courses can help. You cannot start a book on page 1 as a new manager and finish it on page 279 as the complete chief executive. But books and courses put some structure on your random walk, and can help you make sense of the nonsense you encounter.

What growth is and is not

Growth versus training

Michael Phelps won 28 Olympic medals, of which 23 were gold. Behind the glory lay vast amounts of intense training. He was typically swimming up to 80 kilometres a week, in addition to gruelling gym work. As a result, he was consuming up to 12,000 calories a day and sleeping over 8 hours a day. Most of his life was either training or sleeping. He spent less than 1% of his time competing.[163]

At work, you do not have the luxury of training for 99% of the time to perform for 1% of the time. And eating 12,000 calories a day is probably not wise. To make your growth challenge harder, many firms do not like to invest even 1% of your time in training to help you perform in the other 99% of the time. As soon as there is a budget squeeze, training is one of the first items to be cut. The Chartered Institute of Personnel Development (CIPD) ran a survey to find out why training has such low priority.[164] The answers were:

- too busy at work
- family or personal commitments

- insufficient motivation
- resistance from line managers
- insufficient culture of learning at work.

These reasons need a little translation, which I provide below.

- Too busy at work (= not a priority for me).
- Family or personal commitments (= still not a priority for me).
- Insufficient motivation (= in fact, it never will be a priority for me).
- Resistance from line managers (= and it's not a priority for my boss either).
- Insufficient culture of learning at work (= get over it: it's not a priority for anyone).

In theory, firms should be more committed to training. In theory, there should not be war, famine and disease. In the meantime, you have to deal with the world as it is, not the world as it should be. The failure to invest properly in training means that you have to double down on experience as your route to growth, while making the most of whatever formal training and support you can find.

Training can help your growth journey, but it is not a substitute for it. Training is largely controlled by your employer and happens occasionally. Growth is controlled by you and you can access it all the time.

"Deal with the world as it is, not the world as it should be."

Growth versus fixed mindsets

Carol Dweck[165] popularised the idea of fixed and growth mindsets in her book *Mindset*. She focused on education and wanted to discover why some students excelled and others struggled. Her conclusion was that talent was less important than mindset. The right mindset drives the right effort, and that drives success.

The fixed mindset is focused partly on succeeding, but even more on not failing and not looking like a fool in front of your peers.

This really hurts learning. If you praise a child for getting something right, the child learns that praise comes from being right (from not being wrong). So the child will not take on more challenging tasks where it may fail. The child will want to keep on getting praise for succeeding in tasks that it knows are possible.

In contrast, if you praise the child for making effort, regardless of whether they have succeeded or failed, the child learns that effort is what gets praise. This will encourage the child to take risks, push boundaries and keep on learning. This growth mindset links effort and risk taking to success.

Growth beyond the comfort zone

We were all learning to ski on the nursery slopes. Our instructor kept on telling us to "bend ze knees" as we cautiously did our beginner's turns. There was one idiot who kept on trying to do the fancy turns. As a result, she kept on falling over and giving us a good laugh. During the second day, she disappeared from our group, and we thought no more of her.

On the last day, we spotted her again, as she hurtled confidently down the advanced slopes using the advanced turns she had been learning. She had gone beyond her comfort zone to learn, she had taken risks and failed consistently to start with. We had taken no risk and had not learned. She had the growth mindset of taking risks, whereas we had the fixed mindset of avoiding failure.

She learned fast, we learned slow. We started to wonder who the idiots were and who was going to have the last laugh.

Dweck's mindset formula gives rise to two challenges:

- Can this mindset be applied in an adult work environment (as opposed to sports, for instance)?
- How can this mindset be applied? It is not enough to exhort staff to ditch their fixed mindset and have a growth mindset. Failure and looking like a fool in a work setting can have serious negative consequences.

In the rest of this chapter you will discover a practical four-step tool which will allow you to manage your growth journey to achieve your goals.

How to cultivate the habit: the growth cycle

The growth cycle allows you to learn, in real time, from the day-to-day events you experience. It puts structure on the random journey of experience, and helps you make sense of the nonsense you encounter every day. It lets you build your personal success formula for how you can succeed in your context, and lets you keep on adapting your formula as your circumstances change.

In practice, there are four stages to your personal growth cycle. Each stage has its traps and its opportunities:

1. Experience: build the right skills to fuel your career.
2. Reflect: from focus on failure to learning from success.
3. Model: from theory to practice.
4. Test: from your comfort zone to stretch.

These four stages can be captured as a single growth cycle, as shown in Figure 9.1

We will look at how you put this learning cycle to practical use to manage your growth journey.

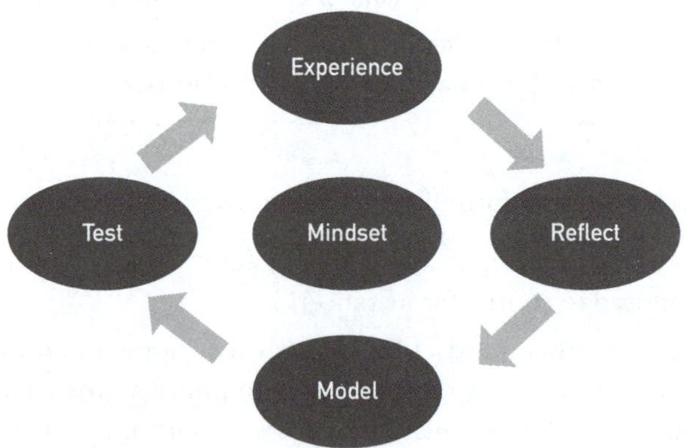

Figure 9.1 The growth cycle[166]

Experience: build the right skills to fuel your career

Experience can be a random walk. If you bump into good experiences, bosses and role models, you accelerate your career. If you find yourself in a dead-end role with negative bosses and role models, you will go nowhere fast. No one else is responsible for your career: you have to make sure that you get the right experiences. Career can be a verb or a noun. You may want to enjoy careering through work from one random experience to another. But if you want your career to be a noun and not a verb, you have to manage it well. You have to turn your random walk of experience into a structured journey of discovery.

> "Career can be a verb or a noun."

Your first and most important task is to work out which skills you want to fuel your career journey. If you cannot be expert at everything, you need a few signature strengths that will differentiate you from your peers. To find out what skills you will need, look at people who are in the sorts of roles you would like have in five to ten years' time. Then reverse engineer their success: the skills that sustain their success are the skills you need to sustain your success.

Exercise 40: build skills for your career

Changes of assignment, role or employer are pivotal moments in any career. It pays to make the right choice. Choosing on the basis of a small uplift in salary is normally a recipe for regret. In coaching clients at key points in their careers, I find that four questions normally help reveal the best solution:

1. **Will I enjoy learning and using these skills?** The growth journey is hard work, and it takes courage to learn new skills. If you do not enjoy your journey, you cannot sustain it: you only excel at what you enjoy.
2. **Will these skills differentiate me from my peers, and will they give me a distinctive claim to fame?** Your real competition as

a manager is not in the marketplace – it is sitting at a hot desk near you competing for the same limited pot of money, management support and promotions. You need to show how you are different and better than your competition.

3. Are these skills fungible? Will you be able to take these skills to other employers, or will they make you totally dependent on your existing employer?
4. Where will I be able to develop these skills best, where are the best projects and the best managers to learn from? How do I now make sure I am assigned to the right projects and managers, or do I need to move firm?

"Your real competition is sitting at a hot desk near you."

Your answers will be, and should be, unique to you. By taking a clear five- to ten-year view of your own development, you take control of your destiny.

Exercise 40 above helps you avoid the main traps of learning from experience:

- **The performance trap.** Many firms value performance over development. One colleague became very good at the deep art of constructing business cases for system integration projects in the insurance industry. This meant she was in great demand for this esoteric skill. The problem was that she hated doing it and there were zero career progression prospects in this arcane art. She scored high on performance and low on development. She resolved the challenge by moving firm and has since flourished.
- **The random walk trap.** As a manager, you encounter an endless stream of random experiences which are a rich source of learning. Value these opportunities to grow. And this is how most managers use experience: they see what comes along and learn from that. You can hope to get lucky with the experiences you encounter, but hope is not a method and luck is not a strategy.

> If you want to succeed, you need to structure your learning journey. Make sure you get the experience you want, not just the experience that fate hands you.

Today, success requires focus, focus and more focus. That means making awkward but clear choices about where you want to take your career. In the past, it was possible to be outstanding in many areas in one lifetime: there was much less knowledge to master. Arguably, the last man to 'know everything' was Thomas Young, who lived from 1773 to 1829. In his time, he claimed to have deciphered the Rosetta Stone, won an argument with Isaac Newton, and become an expert in optics, mathematics, medicine and linguistics. It is inconceivable that anyone can succeed in so many fields today.

"Success requires focus, focus and more focus."

Charles Darwin (1809–92) shows what can be achieved by focus. He was born while Thomas Young was still alive. He spent three years as a gentleman touring the world on a Royal Navy ship, *The Beagle*. Most of his time was spent ashore visiting friends of friends and doing some amateur science. Nothing much seemed to be going on, and nothing much more happened for another 20 years until he was persuaded to publish *On The Origin of Species*.[167] He had spent 20 years focusing on a big idea and working on it. Focus is, increasingly, the key to success.

"If you hate accounting, learn to love accountants."

As the world becomes more complicated, so the need for specialisation increases. Even in the world of leadership, there are too many skills for one person to master. I have mapped out over a hundred skills leaders need: each skill can be broken down into several sub-skills.[168] The good news is that you do not need to master every skill because no leader gets ticks in all the boxes.

Leadership is now a team sport: if you are not expert in one skill, such as accounting, you can always hire plenty of experts in accounting. If you hate accounting, learn to love accountants and bring them on to your team. But every leader has to be good at something, and that requires focus and practice.

"No leader gets ticks in all the boxes."

Reflect: from focus on failure to learning from success

We have all been through the post-mortem, which starts with the question "What went wrong?" which rapidly turns into "Who went wrong?" These tend to be painful but powerful learning events. As human beings, we are hard-wired to focus on avoiding disaster and mistakes. When people talk about learning from experience, they normally mean learning from mistakes. I have heard so many managers talk about all the 'scars on my back' from all the painful learning they have acquired over their career. Learning from mistakes is necessary and painful, but it is rarely done well and it is completely inadequate if you want to learn to succeed. Success is much more than avoiding disaster: it is about having consistent and predictable success.

In practice, most managers are lousy at learning from success. We assume that success is normal and is the natural course of events. Success is neither normal nor natural: it is very hard work. The fact that your presentation went well, or the product was delivered on time, or the sale was made is the result of a long chain of events. If any link in the chain fails, everything fails. So when it all works, it pays to know why it works. If you don't know how you succeeded once, you will not know how to again.

"Most managers are lousy at learning from success."

Learning from success is as important, but less painful, than learning from failure. There is a very simple way you can learn from both success and setbacks, which is effective and painless. You simply have to ask yourself two questions after every significant event. A significant event might be anything from a long presentation to the board to a short but vital phone call. Regardless of how well or poorly the event went, here are your two questions to ask: WWW and EBI. Here they are:

WWW: what went well?

Even in a setback you probably did something that stopped the setback becoming a disaster. This learning is like gold dust: make sure you capture it. Beginning with WWW starts the post-mortem positively. If the event was a success, capture the reasons for the success. You can then add a fourth W to make WWW+W: what worked well and why? Keep on asking the question why to find out the essence of your success.

Eventually, this discipline becomes second nature for both you and your team. When one senior executive left his bank, the CEO stepped up to give a leaving speech and he started by saying: "David, I just want to recap your seven years here by asking WWW: what went well ..." Everyone laughed because WWW was the key tool they had been using for seven years to improve performance. It was ingrained in all they did.

Unlike most self-improvement techniques, WWW is very easy to administer to yourself and your team. You will find you can quietly debrief yourself as you walk down the corridor after coming out of a big meeting. Instead of wasting time ruminating about the meeting, you can use this dead time to build your personal success model.

> **"Create your own secret sauce for success."**

Using WWW consistently allows you to work out what works for you in your context. It is very low on theory but very high on practicality. WWW lets you create your own secret sauce for success. It does not need to work in theory, as long as it works in practice. It will be your own unique success formula.

EBI: even better if

It is easy to reflect on adverse events with WWW's evil twin: what went wrong? If you do this personally, you will land up ruminating and depressing yourself. Telling yourself that you messed up in seven different ways is a good way to ruin your day. Instead, ask yourself EBI: it would have been *even better if* ...

EBI is action-focused, constructive and positive: it forces you to think about what you would do differently and better next time around. Normally, EBI is very simple to say but very hard to do. For instance, when I work with salespeople, they find EBI powerful not just for raising their game, but also for sustaining their game. It is very rare for a salesperson to find an EBI where they think: "It would have been even better if I had really mastered the reverse flip flop power close ..." Normally, their EBIs are much simpler and the most common one is: "It would be even better I talked less and listened more. So it is EBI I focus on asking smart questions instead of thinking about giving smart answers."

EBI is how you can make sure you keep on doing the simple but important things consistently well. Just by doing that, you avoid most of the pitfalls that lead to setbacks.

WWW and EBI is how you can squeeze the most amount of learning from the minimum amount of experience. It is a way of dramatically accelerating your growth journey, without having to rely on going on courses or doing an MBA. As with any new habit, it will feel slightly unnatural to start with. Eventually, it will become second nature and you will find that you cannot stop learning new techniques and reinforcing existing ones.

Exercise 41: reflect to learn from success

Use every significant meeting, call, project or event to learn and grow by debriefing yourself. Ask yourself two questions:

- **WWW:** what went well? Capture yourself succeeding. Learn from success, not just from failure. Build your own unique blueprint for success: discover what works for you in your context.

- **EBI:** even better if ... No matter how well or poorly things went, there will always be things you could do better. Identify them so that you can try them next time.

You can do this exercise as you walk between meetings. To make it really powerful, do the exercise with someone else who was involved in the event. Their independent and objective view will help you discover things that you might miss.

Reflect with your team: use WWW and EBI to raise performance

All good teams debrief regularly. The Red Arrows are intent on delivering the perfect air show every time: they do not want to be better than other air show teams because that is not good enough. They want perfection. That means they debrief after every air show and every practice. In the debrief, the hierarchy is suspended. That means that the most junior person in the room is expected to criticise the most senior, if required. This is essential to any effective team debrief: suspend the hierarchy. If the hierarchy remains in place, team members will say what they think you want to hear, not what you need to hear. It replicates the adult–child relationship where the child is waiting to be praised or punished by the adult. It is not a good relationship to maintain on a team.

Using WWW is a good way to start your team debrief positively, even after an adverse event. WWW shows to the team that this is not the start of the blame game: it is a real opportunity to learn and to improve. By focusing on the positives, you identify what the team can build on instead of focusing on what the team needs to tear down. This positive start to the team debrief sets up a positive dialogue around the setbacks as well.

EBI is a positive and action-focused way of dealing with what went wrong. What went wrong looks backwards and points the blame. EBI looks forwards to how the team as a whole can improve. It forces team members to be constructive, and makes them come up with solutions rather than relying on you to come up with all the solutions.

At this point, I routinely hear executives say: "But we must understand what went wrong. What if one team member is messing it up for the rest of the team?" EBI language allows you to identify what went wrong in an action-focused manner. For instance, one team had a setback when a paper from the team went to the board and it was half-baked. The traditional team debrief would have concluded: "Abdul messed up because it was his paper and he did not let us review it before the board meeting." That is a fairly hostile summary, which will get a rejoinder from Abdul that he was not getting the input and support he needed from the rest of the team. Suddenly, the blame game erupts and no one learns anything.

The EBI approach resulted in a different outcome: "It will be even better if we have a clear timetable for board papers, and for when they will be circulated for review with clear deadlines for who needs to input what by when." The result is a clear timetable and responsibilities that everyone can adhere to in future. Clearly, if some team members then fail to deliver against their responsibilities consistently, that is a performance management issue which the manager can take up.

Exercise 42: reflect with your team to raise performance

Help your team learn and grow by using WWW and EBI as your standard debrief tool. This is just the same as Exercise 41, but done in a group setting, not alone.

The most important trick with this exercise is what you don't do. Never ask about WWW's evil twin, which is "What went wrong?" This exercise is about learning, not about blame.

Model: from theory to practice - using pattern recognition to get smart fast

Go into an airport bookshop and, aside from all the crime thrillers and romantic fiction, you will find a business section. Its shelves will be groaning with the ghost-written autobiographies of successful executives with big egos. They are very keen to tell the whole world not only that they are very successful, but why they succeeded. They believe that their success model is a universal success model: "If you do what I do, you can become as rich, famous and successful as I am" is their key promise. It is a completely false promise, for two reasons.

First, their model of success will be unique to them. What works in setting up a tech venture in Silicon Valley is not what is needed to succeed as a team manager of a clothing manufacturer in Vietnam or in a government department in Germany. Different contexts need different models. There is no universal elixir of leadership that can turn average managers into great leaders. There is only what works for you in your context.

"There is no universal elixir of leadership that can turn average managers into great leaders."

Second, many of the most successful leaders are unique forces of nature. Steve Jobs, the Co-founder of Apple, famously had a 'distortion reality field': he would bend the world and reality to his needs and beliefs. He is also widely credited with being a genius and a jerk.[169] The problem is that people who try to emulate the Jobs' genius and jerk success formula can do the jerk but struggle with being a genius.

We have also seen earlier in this chapter that relying on the random walk of experience is a slow and painful way to build your personal success model, especially as you have to keep changing your model as your career progresses. This means you need some shortcuts to acquire intuition and knowledge fast.

"What leaders do is all about pattern recognition."

The good news is that most of what leaders do is all about pattern recognition: we start to learn how to react to different people and different situations. The even better news is that these situations are so variable, ambiguous and complex that it will be a long time before AI can master them and replace you. For instance:

- When do you step up and when do you step back in a crisis?
- How do you deal with conflict where perhaps three parties are at loggerheads?
- How do you build networks of trust and influence to help you push your agenda?
- How do you persuade someone more powerful than you to change their mind?

Acquiring pattern recognition at speed

William Lever, Founder of Unilever, once said, "I know that half the money I spend on advertising is wasted. My only problem is that I don't know which half."[170] When I first took responsibility for a brand (for P&G), this mattered because most of my budget was my advertising budget.

So the first thing I did was to go into a darkened room. There I watched 50 years of advertising, for Daz, a detergent I was responsible for. It was like watching a social history of Britain. It started with black and white advertising, which lasted an interminable 90 seconds, through to punchy 30-second and even 20-second blasts. Each piece of advertising had been researched to see how well it was remembered the day after airing (this is called DAR research): if it is not remembered, it is not effective.

By the end of a long day in the film room, I was able to predict, with uncanny accuracy, how well each piece of advertising would score in the DAR. This was not about advertising genius, it was about acquiring pattern recognition at speed.

Such pattern recognition is now embedded in algorithms, which can even predict which songs are likely to become hits and are worth promoting, and which will not make the grade. It is not about musical insight, it is all about pattern recognition. Leadership is pattern recognition under highly ambiguous and complex conditions, which are beyond the reach of AI for the foreseeable future.

Exercise 43: use pattern recognition

Learning what works through trial and error is risky and time-consuming. You need some simple ways of accelerating your learning. You need to reach out and get some help. Here are three ways you can acquire pattern recognition at speed:

1. Buy the book or go on the course. Neither the book nor the course will give you the perfect answer. But they should give you some principles that will let you test what works for you.
2. Find an internal mentor who can guide you and advise you. A good mentor will help you understand what works in difficult situations in your context. They can advise on best practice, not on best theory. They can also guide you towards the right assignments and experiences, which will help your career.
3. Find an external coach. A good one will have seen the patterns of success and failure in countless other firms, and can ask the right questions to help you discover what works for you.

Portraits of resilience: learning

Mark Evans, explorer and Founder of Outward Bound Oman

Mark's idea of a gentle weekend is a trip into the middle of the desert. For most people, this would be a major expedition into the unknown, but Mark handles it as easily as most people handle a trip to the shops. Tackling sand dunes, navigating the way, deflating and inflating tyres, having the right kit and setting up camp is child's play when you have led expeditions across the Arctic and across the Empty Quarter of Arabia, by camel.

Mark became comfortable in extreme environments through constant learning. But it is not learning you can get from a textbook; when you fall through the ice in the Arctic far from any help, Google will not save you. In his words, "Learning is an apprenticeship where you learn from people who are far, far better than you are, and they give you the confidence and tools to deal with the unexpected.

Comfort zones are all relative, and you have to keep pushing your comfort zone. But you cannot climb Everest if you have not climbed smaller mountains first. It is an apprenticeship." In practice, Mark was learning about extreme environments the same way that leaders learn about the office environment: not from textbooks, but from role models and from experience.

Mark has now become the role model for the next generation. He set up the University of the Desert to bring together youth from different cultures. He has also set up and runs Outward Bound Oman. Although teaching, he still learns from every expedition: crossing the Empty Quarter he learned that ceremonial camels generously loaned by royalty really do not like the hard work of being in the desert.

Mark's layers of resilience include strong accountability (Chapter 7) and self-efficacy (Chapter 4), which matters when things go wrong and you are on the edge: "Always have a Plan A, B, C and D" says Mark. Not everyone enjoys living on the edge, but he does. He also knows that his resilience is dependent on context and culture (Chapter 10): "Don't ask me to sell double glazing!" he pleads.

Test: move from your comfort zone to stretch zone

All sport is brutal. There is no hiding place and, in the end, you either win or lose. Rugby is especially brutal because of the intensity and high physical contact. There are few achievements more outstanding than winning the Grand Slam: beating every other nation in the annual Six Nations Championship. For Scotland, a relatively small country in terms of population, to achieve this is highly unusual. The last time Scotland achieved this feat was in 1990. The captain at the time was David Sole, and he recalled the pressure: "It was the amateur era. That meant on Monday morning you went back to work and, if you had had a bad match, everyone would tell you all about it. The pressure did not end with the final whistle: it was with you all the time."[171]

The way David Sole, under coach Jim Tefler, prepared Scotland for victory was the way that all successful sports teams prepare. Of course, the training was intense. But the really important part of the training happened at the end, when they were all tired. That is when they went through all their key routines and key techniques one more time. As David Sole observed: "Anyone can execute the routines when they are fresh and under no pressure. What matters is executing the routines when you are tired and under pressure."

A thousand kilometres away in Lympstone, the Royal Marine Commandos have their training base. Officers go through an 15-month gruelling training regime to earn the coveted green beret.[172] Just like the rugby team, the real tests come when they are all already exhausted and at the point of collapse: that is when more is asked of them, and that is when they have to show good judgement in decision making. But the training is carefully calibrated. Recruits are not thrown in at the deep end. Before they start, they are given a 12-week training programme[173] to follow to get them up to speed. Week one sounds easy: start by jogging two miles at eleven minutes a mile. Grandpa can do that, on a good day. You should also carry a 5kg load for one mile. Grandma can do that on most days.

By week 12, you should be able to run 4 miles at 7 minutes 30 seconds a mile, and carry a 15kg load for 4 miles. Neither grandpa nor grandma would look forward to that. And, at that point, you are ready to start the real training. By the end of your 15 months of training, you will be enjoying the dubious pleasure of a 30-mile self-directed march across the moors with full gear (up to 60kg) in just 8 hours.[174]

Sports, military and business share some common characteristics when it comes to effective training. The most important principle is the one that the Royal Marines push hard: "Train smart, not hard." Training hard simply pushes you to break down. Training smart is partly about having directed and supported training: you cannot become a great rugby team or a Royal Marine by trusting to the random walk of experience.

"Train smart, not hard."

The other part of training smart, not hard, is about testing and pushing your limits. There is clearly a trade-off here: if you do not push yourself, you never learn and grow. If you push yourself too hard too fast, you simply break down. And this is as true of business as it is of sports or Marines.

Look at the figure below and think about when you have learned the most and achieved the most. It is unlikely to have been when you were in your comfort zone. Easy street is important, because that is where you can rest and recover when you have pushed too hard. Equally, when you are in the stress zone, you may well have been surviving, not thriving.

Your comfort zone is a very dangerous place to be. This is where you can perform well, and your employer will probably be delighted with your performance. But your career is not just about performance, it is also about development and growth. You have to keep on learning and growing. When you are in your comfort zone, you are not pushing yourself to learn, grow or develop. You sacrifice your future development for performance today.

"Your comfort zone is a very dangerous place to be."

Most people thrive when they are in their stretch zone. This is when you have to push yourself, you have to learn and adapt and you are at the edge of your competence. There may well be

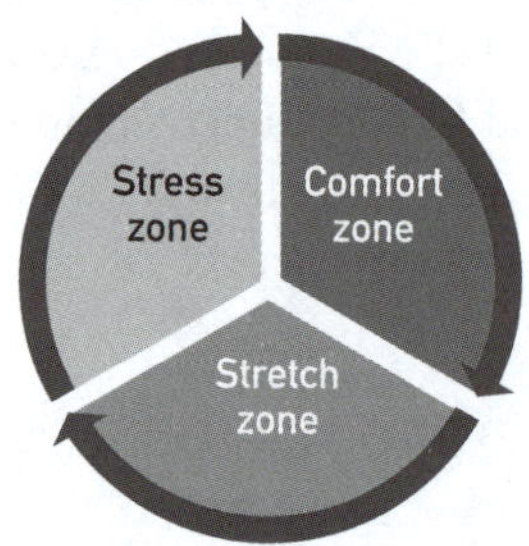

Figure 9.2 Find your zone

pressure, but you can handle it because you are under control. The critical difference between pressure and stress is control. When you face a challenging task and tight deadline, that is clearly pressure. But now take away your ability to control the outcome, become dependent on others who may not share your sense of urgency, and perhaps both the timing and the deliverables change at the last moment. When you lose control like that, pressure becomes stress. Under stress conditions you are simply in survival mode.

Exercise 44: move from your comfort zone to stretch zone

As you manage your learning journey, you have to keep on pushing your limits to learn new skills and new ways of doing things. Here is how you can stretch yourself without breaking yourself:

- *Be clear about what you want to achieve.* Do you have goals that demand you stretch yourself and grow or are you living in your comfort zone?
- *Start simple and keep making incremental gains.* If you need to learn public speaking, your first attempt should not be a keynote speech to a big conference. Start simple: perhaps a three-minute presentation to a team of three colleagues. You can slowly extend your speech and your audience.
- *Keep learning from experience, good or bad.* Use WWW and EBI as described in Exercise 42.
- *Get help and support.* All top performers get help from coaches, trainers or mentors who will help them structure their learning so it is deliberate, measured and effective. If you have no coach, use books, courses and videos.

This is how the Royal Marines Commandos[175] stretch and grow recruits: train smart, not hard, get support, build your skills step by step and have a clear goal. You can do the same.

Summary

You have to keep on learning and growing if you are to flourish, or even survive, a 45-year career marathon. The skills you have today have a limited shelf life:

- You need new skills as your career progresses. You need technical skills at the start of your career, and you need people and political skills as you advance.
- There will always be someone younger, hungrier and lower cost ready to do your job: you have to learn new skills to stay ahead.
- Any technical skills you have are under threat from AI, and from the changing needs of your industry.
- The future of your employment depends on your employability. If other firms do not want your talent, how long will your existing employer want your talent?

You are responsible for your own growth and development. We live in a world where average job tenure is just six years, so you have to ensure that you remain employable over your career. To manage your growth, use the growth cycle:

- **Experience:** make sure you get the right assignments that will let you build the sorts of skills you will need in five to ten years ahead. Manage your development, not just your performance. Convert your random walk of experience into a structured journey of discovery.
- **Reflect:** Learn from successes as well as from setbacks. The key is to use WWW (what went well), before you ask EBI (even better if). This is action-focused and positive. You can use it for yourself, and you can also use it to debrief with your team after every significant event.
- **Model:** Reach out and get some help, so that you can put some structure on your journey of discovery. Use books, courses, mentors and coaches to give you frameworks that can help you make sense of the nonsense you encounter, and that will let you acquire pattern recognition at speed. Most of leadership is about clear and quick pattern recognition, which helps you respond well to difficult situations.

- **Test:** Get out of your comfort zone, which is great for short-term performance but does not help you with your long-term development. Train smart, not hard. Test your limits one small step at a time. If you go into the stress zone, you will break down and you will need to recover by going back into your comfort zone for a while.

Chapter 10

Find your sanctuary: the power of culture

Bank robber Willy Sutton was asked why he robbed banks. "Because that is where the money is,"[176] he replied. If you want money, go where the money is. If you want power, go where the power is. If you want fame, go where the fame is. If you want to build resilience, go where they build resilience.

We are all creatures of circumstance, so it pays to choose the right circumstances. This chapter shows how you can identify the right sort of firm and context to help you flourish, build resilience and perform well.

Chapter 8 showed that you can build your internal resilience through a sense of purpose, autonomy, supportive relationships and mastery. This chapter shows that your internal journey needs to be mirrored by an external environment, which allows you to build purpose, autonomy, supportive relationships and mastery.

Why culture matters

A constant theme of this book is that resilience is contextual. Most office workers would feel low resilience if suddenly abandoned in the middle of the Amazonian jungle. But, equally, the explorers and mountaineers we have encountered in this book would feel deeply uncomfortable in an office environment.

The power of context became clear when we invited the CEO of a major bank to teach a sample lesson at one of the schools that

Teach First serves. In theory, it was an easy task. He was going to teach a lesson about money. A bank boss should know about money. In the same week that the lesson was scheduled, he also had a global board meeting. Not surprisingly, that weekend he found himself hard at work. The surprise was that he was not worried about the board meeting: he was in his comfort zone there. He was fretting anxiously about his school lesson. He knew how to deal with grizzled bank executives, but he had no clue how to deal with disaffected teenagers from a deprived community. He had deep resilience in a banking context and low resilience for working in a school context.

As part of the deal with Teach First, the CEO then invited the Teach First teacher who hosted his visit to do a presentation to the board of his bank. The teacher, who was highly resilient in the face of the challenges of teaching in an inner-city school, was quietly terrified of presenting to all the grizzled bank executives.

"We perform at our best only if we are in our right context."

The reality is that we perform at our best only if we are in our right context. As an employee, you have to find the context where you can flourish. As a manager, you have to create the context in which your team can flourish.

"Too many organisations help extraordinary people achieve very ordinary things."

Too many organisations help extraordinary people achieve very ordinary things. You are invited to hang your coat, ambition and creativity in the cloakroom on arrival at work each morning. But not all organisations are like that. Some organisations produce alchemy where they help relatively normal people achieve abnormally, for better or for worse. We tend to rise or sink to the level of expectation and behaviour around us. It is very hard to buck the trend.

Where you work or study, and the company you choose, may not decide your destiny, but it will certainly shape it. You cannot choose your school, but you can choose where to work and where to live.

The case examples that follow illustrate the power of place. Choosing the right place leads to sustainable high performance and builds resilience. Choosing the wrong place makes it easy to underachieve and to be led astray.

The tale of two schools

What do the following have in common?

Ten Olympic gold medal winners, one Nobel Prize Laureate, the Kings of Nepal and Jordan, novelist George Orwell, Oscar winner Eddie Redmayne, economist John Maynard Keynes, Napoleon's nemesis the Duke of Wellington, fictional spy James Bond and real spy and traitor Guy Burgess, two winning teams of the FA Cup, explorer Bear Grylls, 19 British prime ministers, the Archbishop of Canterbury, scientist Robert Boyle (creator of Boyle's Law) and 37 recipients of the Victoria Cross (out of 1,358 granted for the highest valour in conflict).[177]

The answer is that they all went to the same secondary school just outside London: Eton College. The walls of the school exude the expectation that you will succeed, somehow.

Twelve kilometres closer to Central London is another secondary school, in Ealing. Its main claim to fame came when its pupils featured in riots in 2011, which lead to looting, arson and five deaths. The school is at the end of the tube line. When I visited, I found that under half the pupils had ever been into the centre of London. It was a foreign country to them. When I asked what they wanted to do after they left school, many girls said they wanted to become models, many boys said that they wanted to become footballers. But it was already too late: poor diet and lack of training meant that they were unlikely to achieve their goals. They suffered from a poverty of aspiration and support.

It is easier to have high aspirations when you are surrounded by high expectations. And it is easier to succeed in achieving your dreams when you are surrounded by successful role models, and you have the support and networks to chase your dreams.

At its simplest, you are most likely to sustain high performance in a highly challenging but highly supportive environment. High-performing organisations normally combine challenge and support, and they can by very attractive destinations for new graduates in the job market, even if the pay is not high.

The Royal Marines Commandos and many sports teams offer high challenge and high support. They do not simply demand performance and resilience, they help you build it with intense support.

In contrast, there are plenty of organisations that offer high challenge but low support. These are 'burn and churn' firms. Historically, investment banks (and some top law firms) would hire top talent at top salaries and then expect top performance. They screen for resilience and they expect you to bring your resilience to the job: they are not there to help you build your resilience. This is a pressure cooker world in which only the fittest survive.

Despite the ravages of global competition, there are still low challenge organisations. One such organisation had a near monopoly on part of the global payments system. It was the classic country club. The headquarters was a modern palace in a leafy park, working hours were short, pay was high and the café served the finest food and wine at lunchtime. It was a joy to work at if you wanted to retire while still at work. It attracted people who wanted

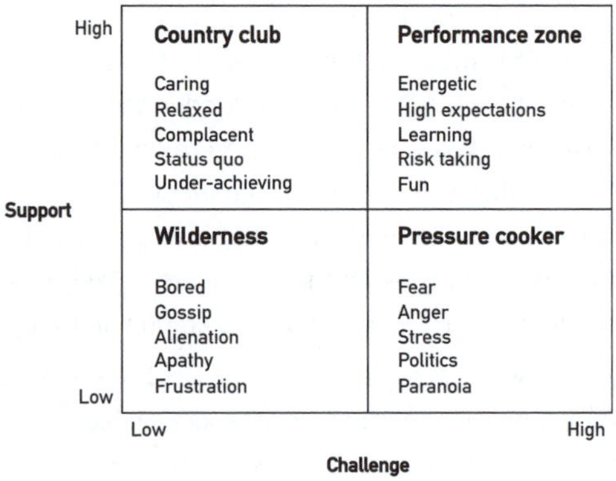

Support	Challenge: Low	Challenge: High
High	**Country club** Caring Relaxed Complacent Status quo Under-achieving	**Performance zone** Energetic High expectations Learning Risk taking Fun
Low	**Wilderness** Bored Gossip Alienation Apathy Frustration	**Pressure cooker** Fear Anger Stress Politics Paranoia

Figure 10.1 Find your sanctuary

that lifestyle, so the culture became relaxed, complacent and very gossipy. They were not the sort of people who would last long in an inner-city school room, an investment bank trading floor or in the Royal Marines. Their survival depended on the survival of the firm's global monopoly, not on their personal resilience.

Where you work shapes you and your future.

The tale of two towns

Tsubame and Sanjo are a pair of nondescript towns about 250 kilometres north of Tokyo. At first sight, they are unremarkable. But go into them, and you will find yourself in the middle of Japan's metalworking world. Over 80% of Japan's domestic metal work is produced in the area. It is easy to see why: the two towns are a cauldron of expertise and innovation. They take great pride in being the best.

Being the best is not easy. It takes five years for an apprentice to become competent enough to make basic goods that can be sold. To achieve real mastery takes decades. For instance, after five decades of work, Mizuochi Ryoichi is the recognised master of making razor blades: he has a three-year waiting list for his work. Kondo Kazutoshi focuses only on making hoes, which may sound like a limited product line-up, but he has over a thousand different sorts of hoe. Different regions, different soils and different crops need different sorts of hoe and he works to produce precisely the right sort of hoe for each need. Nearby, Hinoura Tsukasa is recognised as a Master of Japanese Traditional Crafts by the Japanese Government. He makes exquisite kitchen knives, which can sell for thousands of dollars each.[178]

Of course, it would be possible for these craftsmen to exist anywhere. But, in practice, they all co-exist in one place where they can exchange ideas, compete with each other and produce the talent for the next generation. Because of their expertise, customers come here, which means that the craftsmen learn more about what customers really need and want. This creates a positive feedback loop: more expertise brings in more customers which drives up expertise. Supply and demand drive each other.[179]

City clusters of expertise exist everywhere. Even within a city, clusters emerge. In London, the insurance district sits to the east of the Bank of England, and the banking industry is clustered around the other sides of the Bank of England. Both hubs exist inside just one square mile of land. Hatton Garden is famous for its jewellers, Oxford Street for its shopping, the West End for its theatres, Shoreditch for its start-ups, Saville Row for bespoke tailors, Old Street for web firms, Soho for post-production services and Fleet Street used to be the centre of the newspaper world. Of course, there are theatres, jewellers, banks and tailors elsewhere in London, but each trade has a cluster of top talent.

Place does not dictate your destiny, but it helps to shape it.

"Place does not dictate your destiny, but it helps to shape it."

How to cultivate the habit

The high challenge and high support organisation is a good start towards building resilience and sustaining high performance. But you cannot rely on your employer to provide all the challenge and support for you. You have to craft your role appropriately, as a manager, and you have to understand how to build appropriate challenge and support for your team. In practice, there are four pillars you need to build to sustain high performance:[180]

1. Autonomy
2. Support
3. Mastery
4. Purpose

It is worth seeing what is not there. The invisible can be as useful as the visible. There is nothing about extrinsic motivators such as pay, rewards and working conditions. These do nothing to build resilience. Many of the organisations with the most resilient staff have poor pay: the church and armed forces, for instance. Sustained motivation and resilience are intrinsic, not extrinsic: it comes from within. But autonomy, support, mastery and purpose are easier to find in some roles than others. If you know what you are looking for, you can find the sort of role that will allow you to discover your motivation and build your resilience.

"Sustained motivation and resilience is intrinsic, not extrinsic."

To understand how you can craft these aspects of work, we will look at one case example in depth and refer to a few others.

"You can train skills, but you cannot train values."

Portraits of resilience: culture

Natasha Porter, Founder and CEO of Unlocked

Traditionally, prison officers have not attracted top graduates. The government is clear that "you don't need qualifications to become a prison officer".[181] Natasha wanted to ensure that even those with top qualifications should see the prison officer role as a real option. This would support the government's drive to tackle the cost and damage of prisoner re-offending. Too often, rehabilitation can take second place in the prison service where pressure to simply run the regime can mean security processes come first. Rehabilitation requires dealing with mental health and drug issues, enabling learning and skills building, as well as maintaining order.

To achieve these ambitious goals, Natasha developed Unlocked to attract top graduates and to build a distinctive culture. Graduates are selected not just for skills, but for values as well: it is easier to train skills when people already have the right values. Unlocked went back to first principles in developing a training programme for its graduates. This taught the basic skills of being a prison officer, but also created a distinct esprit de corps among each cohort of graduates who trained together. They are placed in prisons in groups of 10–12: this is the minimum effective size to maintain the culture of the group. They are also mentored by supportive senior prison officers, so that they do not revert to the run the regime mentality. It can be easy for new staff to be swamped by existing culture, but if they are going to have a chance to affect change, their new approaches and attitudes need to be protected and nurtured.

Natasha exhibits many of the other characteristics of deep resilience: she is passionate about her mission (Chapter 8), has a high degree of self-efficacy (Chapter 4) and is a good example of putting emotion to work (Chapter 2). Her anger at the obvious injustices of the justice system spurred her to start Unlocked.

Unlocked shows the power of the right framework to help build and sustain resilience. Unlocked aims to reform prisons, reduce violence and reduce re-offending by hiring great graduates to become great prison officers. Natasha Porter started Unlocked in 2016 and her first cohort of graduates started in prison in 2017. The success of the programme has been instant and it has grown rapidly. Its success depends on building a distinctive culture which is not just about control and run the regime but also about rehabilitation. Unlocked displays the four pillars of high-performing groups: autonomy, support, mastery and purpose. Each element is baked into the design of the Unlocked programme:

Autonomy

Autonomy is vital for motivation and resilience. If you are simply a cog in a machine with no discretion, it is hard to sustain effort for long. Autonomy is important for anyone, not just high-flying professionals who expect to act independently. Even on the floor of car factories, it is now routine to see operators being given far more autonomy than ever: they manage their own performance data and can control the line when necessary.

Unlocked graduates are given a high degree of responsibility from the start. They work regular shifts during which they are likely to be in charge of a prison wing where they might have responsibility for up to 100 prisoners. What comes with autonomy is both responsibility and risk, as the first cohort of graduate officers soon discovered. One had to take responsibility for dealing with a suicide she discovered, while another had the dubious distinction of being potted by a prisoner. Being potted means that a prisoner decides to pour a pot of their urine over your head.

“What comes with autonomy is both responsibility and risk.”

Support

Autonomy without support is the Darwinian world of survival of the fittest. The right support helps you through the hard times.

Support for the hard times is vital and is built into the Unlocked programme. Graduates are not placed in prisons evenly across the country. They are placed in cohorts of eight to twelve graduates per prison, so that there is an immediate peer group for them to rely on. They all have a WhatsApp group, which is very active. This support came into its own after the potting and suicide events. In both cases, the graduate was flooded with support: from their mentor, colleagues and other graduates on the programme. Being part of a supportive community is a massive aid to resilience.

“Being part of a supportive community is a massive aid to resilience.”

Mastery

Unlocked graduates start with an intensive six-week summer institute before starting work. Natasha Porter describes this training as the chance to “embed muscle memory in procedures”. Only when the basics become routine can you focus your mental energy on the more complex and demanding parts of the job, such as dealing with unexpected and potentially dangerous situations. This is the same in any role: making the basics routine frees you up to focus on the bigger challenge. For the same reason, the ambulance service has strict and set routines about exactly how all their equipment is laid out: it is the same in every ambulance. Each crew knows exactly what to expect, and does not have to waste time or effort thinking about the basics. They can focus on the emergency.

Unlocked's support for mastery continues over the two years of the programme. They receive another six weeks of training, including meetings with an assigned mentor every fortnight, regular group workshops where they share and solve common challenges, completion of an MSc programme and formal training at a second-year summer institute. It is not possible to sustain high performance or to have resilience if you do not have competence. Organisations that help you build mastery also help you build resilience.

Although your employer can help you achieve mastery, this is a journey you have to want to take. Unlocked tests for this. They put participants through role plays in a mock-up cell with an actor: regardless of how well or badly they do on their first attempt, the real test is how well they do on their second effort. They need to show that they hear feedback and that they are ready to act on it.

Purpose

You have to be clear in your own mind what your true purpose is. You have to find the context or firm that fits your purpose. The firm will not change for you, and you will find it hard to change for the firm. You have to find the right fit before you join. If there is fit, you will enjoy the work and you will naturally find the resilience to keep going in the face of adversity. If there is no fit, you will struggle.

With a true sense of purpose comes both enjoyment and resilience. If you enjoy what you do, you are far more likely to stick at it through hard times as well as good times.

Picking the right context is your responsibility. If you are in the wrong context, it is your responsibility to do something about it. There is no right or wrong context, there is only the context that plays to your strengths and preferences. Until you know yourself, you cannot know where you want to work. In practice, this means that many people in their twenties go through several employers.

Average tenure for 25 to 34 years olds is just 2.8 years, versus 10.1 years for 55 to 64 year olds.[182] Finding your context takes time, and you need to take care you do not fall into the wrong place early: it can be hard to escape.

Destiny and the dark side of place

Just as positive places encourage positive behaviours, so negative behaviour encourages negative behaviour. For instance, the Hofstad Group was a violent terrorist group based in the Netherlands. It managed to kill film director Theo van Gogh and was plotting attacks on Parliament, nuclear reactors and Schiphol Airport. After the group was broken up and jailed, the Dutch decided to investigate the motives of the group members. Many had been influenced by the echo chamber of the internet and social media: self-selecting groups tend to reinforce each other's views and take them to extremes in the pursuit of approval from the rest of the group. The planning and use of violence were driven less by ideology and more by the need for approval from the group.[183]

In similar fashion, the European Commission found that members of extreme and often violent racist groups were driven mainly by the need for identity, belonging, excitement and purpose. The actual ideology was a symptom, not a cause of their violence.[184]

Choose your place carefully; nowadays, your place is often on the web.

Exercise 45: build a resilient culture

Too many managers think that building resilient teams is a mandate to mismanage: they hope that a resilient team can tolerate the stress and pressure of being badly managed. True resilience is about helping your team thrive and sustain high performance in the long term. To do this, you need to apply to your team the same four principles you applied to yourself in Exercise 39. This exercise helps you find a context where you will sustain your own motivation. It also helps you build the intrinsic motivation, performance and resilience of your team.

Ask yourself what you are doing to help your team build the four pillars of sustained high performance:

1. **Autonomy:** do you delegate everything you can?
2. **Support:** do you help and support your team, or do you monitor and micro-manage them?
3. **Mastery:** do you act as coach to your team, or do you solve every problem for them? Do you give them stretching assignments and relevant training?
4. **Purpose:** can you show that your team makes a meaningful and worthwhile contribution?

Summary

Where you work shapes you and your future. Some places demand resilience, other places help you build your resilience. We all rise or fall to the level of expectations around us. If you are to flourish, you need to find a place that has a combination of high challenge, aspirations and high support.

Chapter 8 showed how you can build your internal resilience by finding your purpose. Your purpose will be reinforced by building autonomy, supportive relationships and mastery. This chapter shows that you will flourish in a context that provides you with purpose, autonomy, mastery and supportive relationships. Your internal journey should be supported by your external environment.

"Some places demand resilience, other places help you build your resilience."

An organisation that will help you build resilience will offer you four pillars of strength:

- **Autonomy:** you will have high accountability and responsibility. You will not be micro-managed and monitored in detail.

- **Support:** you will have formal and informal networks of support to help you through the hard times.
- **Mastery:** the firm will be committed to helping you achieve mastery of your craft through formal training, mentoring, peer group support and appropriately challenging opportunities to help you stretch and learn.
- **Purpose:** there will be a fit between your motivation and the needs of the firm, and you will be able to build on your strengths and enjoy the work for what it is.

Ultimately, it is your responsibility to find the context which works for you. As a manager, you also have a responsibility to ensure that these four pillars are in place for your team, so that they can flourish as well.

"It is your responsibility to find the context which works for you."

Conclusion: choose your path

The good news is that you do not need to be born resilient. You can develop your resilience. There is no magic pill which will make you resilient. Instead, there are many tried and tested techniques which will help you become more resilient. You do not need to use every technique. Start out by focusing on one or two core themes. As a recovering pessimist, my life was transformed by focusing on some of the techniques for becoming more optimistic. You can focus on other techniques: reaching out, FAST thinking, dealing with negative emotions or managing your energy. You do not have to master every technique to become resilient. Mastering just one technique at a time can be life-changing.

Behind every technique there is a simple principle: the power of choice. You always have a choice about what you do, how you feel and how you will react in any situation. The challenge is that most of the time we work on autopilot, which means your choices are unconscious, not conscious. Most of the time, your autopilot serves you well and makes it easy to deal with the complexity and challenges of day-to-day life. But, sometimes, it will let you down.

"You always have choices, even if they are uncomfortable choices."

Learning resilience is about making conscious choices about what you do and how you feel. The first great step is to know that you always have choices, even if they are uncomfortable choices. Knowing that you always have choice is empowering and liberating. You do not have to have your feelings and actions dictated to you. You do not have to feel angry, upset or pessimistic: those are choices. That means challenging the assumptions on which your autopilot works whenever it lets you down. You do not need to abandon your autopilot: you simply need to help it improve so that it helps you reliably in every situation.

The tools of resilience will help you in any context anywhere. But there will be some contexts where you need to be, and will be, more resilient. Being resilient in your chosen career is vital to sustain high performance over many years. This means you have to choose your context well: make sure you work in the right role with the right team in the right firm. You will know that you have the right context if you enjoy what you do.

> "Whatever your journey is, enjoy it."

Enjoyment is the final, vital secret of resilience. You only excel at what you enjoy. Achieving excellence takes a huge amount of discretionary effort, which you can only sustain if you enjoy what you do. So, whatever your journey is, enjoy it.

Notes

Introduction

1. The big five personality traits are openness, neuroticism, agreeableness, extraversion and conscientiousness. The model was first advanced by Ernest Tupes and Raymond Christal in 1961.
2. Ivcevic, Z. (2014) 'Predicting school success: Comparing Conscientiousness, Grit, and Emotion Regulation Ability', *Journal of Research in Personality*, 52, pp. 29–36.
3. The programmes referenced are Foundations of Positive Psychology at the University of Pennsylvania and Harvard Neuroscience MCB80x. Both are excellent.

Chapter 1

4. Danner, D.D., Snowdon, D.A. and Friesen, W.V. (2001) 'Positive emotions in early life and longevity: Findings from the nun study', *Journal of Personality and Social Psychology*, 80(5), pp. 804–13, available at: http://dx.doi.org/10.1037/0022-3514.80.5.804.
5. Based on comparing top and bottom quartile for positive emotions expressed.
6. https://blogs.scientificamerican.com/beautiful-minds/is-an-optimistic-mind-associated-with-a-healthy-heart/.
7. Dr Johannes Eichstaedt's work at the University of Pennsylvania, focusing on big data psychology.
8. 'Predictive power' is obviously sub-optimal phrasing, but the language is easier than referring to Pearson *r*, which is technically more accurate.
9. Case, A. and Deaton, A. (2015) 'Rising morbidity and mortality in midlife among white non-Hispanic Americans in the 21st century', *PNAS*, 8 December, 112 (49), pp. 15078–83.
10. Kim, E.S., et al. (2016) 'Optimism and Cause-Specific Mortality: A Prospective Cohort Study', *American Journal of Epidemiology*, pp. 1–9.
11. Kohut, M.L., Cooper, M.M., Nickolaus, M.S., Russell, D.R., Cunnick, J.E. (2002) 'Exercise and psychosocial factors modulate

immunity to influenza vaccine in elderly individuals', *Journals of Gerontology Series A Biological Sciences and Medical Sciences*, September 2002, 57(9): pp. M557–62.

12. Seligman, M. (1998) *Learned Optimism: How to Change Your Mind and Your Life*, Chapter 6, Pocket Books.
13. An interview I did, first quoted in (2015). *The Mindset of Success: Accelerate Your Career from Good Manager to Great Leader*, Kogan Page.
14. Robison, J. (2007) 'It pays to be optimistic. Exploring the connections between optimism and business success', *Gallup Business Journal*, 9 August, available at: news.gallup.com/businessjournal/28303/pays-optimistic.aspx.
15. https://www.forbes.com/sites/tykiisel/2012/10/16/65-of-americans-choose-a-better-boss-over-a-raise-heres-why/\#289a3be776d2. This research by Michelle McQuaid is not peer-reviewed, but is widely quoted and believable.
16. Barclays Equity Gilt study 2018, available at: https://www.investmentbank.barclays.com/news/2018-equity-gilt-study.html.
17. John Toth and Proinsias O'Mahony: https://www.irishtimes.com/business/personal-finance/optimism-pays-better-than-pessimism-1.3166507.
18. The S&P hit 757 in March 2009 and 2,862 in August 2018, excluding the effect of dividend payouts.
19. Kahneman, D. (2012) *Thinking, Fast and Slow*. Penguin, 2012.
20. STIR Education is a not-for-profit organisation, which I chair. It is currently working mainly in India and Uganda.
21. Maslow, A.H. (1943) 'A theory of human motivation', *Psychological Review*, 50 (4), pp. 370–96 : DOI:10.1037/h0054346 – via psychclassics.yorku.ca.
22. Collins, J. (2001) *Good to Great*. Random House.
23. Emperor Ming decides to force a marriage with heroine Dale. Two banners announce the marriage: the first proclaims, "All creatures will make merry" and the second "Under pain of death".
24. Brickman, P. and Coates, D. (1978) 'Lottery Winners and Accident Victims: Is Happiness Relative?', *Journal of Personality and Social Psychology*, Vol. 36, No. 8, pp. 917–27.
25. Wildeman, C. Turney, K. and Schnit, J. (2014), 'The Hedonic Consequences of Punishment Revisited', *Journal of Criminal Law and Criminology*, Vol. 104,Issue 1, Article 4, Winter.
26. Wang, R., Yang, F. and Haigh, M.M. (2017),'Let me take a selfie: Exploring the psychological effects of posting and viewing selfies and groupies on social media', *Telematics and Informatics*, Volume 34, Issue 4, July, pp. 274–83.

27. Davila, J., etal., (2012) 'Frequency and Quality of Social Networking Among Young Adults: Associations With Depressive Symptoms, Rumination, and Corumination', *Psychology of Popular Media Culture,* 1 April, 1(2), pp. 72–86, DOI: 10.1037/a0027512.
28. Primack, B.A., et al. (2017) 'Use of multiple social media platforms and symptoms of depression and anxiety: A nationally-representative study among U.S. young adults', *Computers in Human Behavior,* Volume 69, April, pp 1–9.
29. Kuss, D.J. Orc, I.D. and Griffiths, M.D. (2011)'Online Social Networking and Addiction – A Review of the Psychological Literature', *International Journal of Environmental Research and Public Health,* 8(9).
30. Sean Parker has been widely quoted on hacking the brain, see: http://calnewport.com/blog/2017/11/10/sean-parker-on-facebooks-brain-hacking/.
31. http://unesdoc.unesco.org/images/0026/002603/260382e.pdf.
32. Wiseman, R. (2003) *The Luck Factor: Changing Your Luck, Changing Your Life – The Four Essential Principles,* Miramax books.
33. This quote has also been attributed to Gary Player, Lee Trevino and many other golfing legends. All that is clear is that it seems to be a golfing quotation ... maybe.
34. For more on this, see one of my other books: *How to Influence and Persuade,* Pearson, 2012.

Chapter 2

35. Neuroscientists have located the source of this disorder, which is in the voltage-gated sodium channel SCN9A. It can affect whole families. See Minde, J.K. (2006) 'Norrbottnian congenital insensitivity to pain', *Acta Orthopaedica,* 77: sup 321, pp. 1–32, DOI: 10.1080/17453690610046495a.
36. Medical Research Council Insight: https://www.insight.mrc.ac.uk/2014/02/27/painless-a-q-a-with-geoff-woods/. See also the BBC story about Stefan Betz: http://www.bbc.com/future/story/20170426-the-people-who-never-feel-any-pain.
37. This was the description of nineteenth-century romantic poet Lord Byron, by Lady Caroline Lamb. It could have been a compliment.
38. Baibak, P. and Hare, R.D. (2006) *Snakes in Suits: When Psychopaths Go to Work.* HarperCollins.
39. *Othello,* Act III, Scene iii.
40. Dealing with fears is dealt with very well in Peters, S. (2012) *The Chimp Paradox: The Mind Management Programme to Help You Achieve Success, Confidence and Happiness.* Vermilion.

Chapter 3

41. Kahneman, D. (2011) *Thinking, Fast and Slow*. Farrow, Strauss and Giroux.

42. Seligman, M. (2017) *Authentic Happiness: Using the New Positive Psychology to Realise Your Potential for Lasting Fulfilment*. Hodder & Stoughton Limited.

Chapter 4

43. Gandhi, L. (2013) 'A History Of 'Snake Oil Salesmen', National Public Radio, 26 August.

44. https://en.wikipedia.org/wiki/File:SnakeOilDecision.jpg.

45. The king of self-efficacy is a professor at Stanford University: Albert Bandura. For a summary, see: https://www.uky.edu/~eushe2/Bandura/Bandura1994EHB.pdf.

46. The king of locus control is Julian Rotter (1916–2014) at the University of Connecticut. Read his (1954) *Social Learning and Clinical Psychology*, Prentice-Hall.

47. VUCA was first described by Warren Bennis and Burt Nanis in *Leaders: Strategies for Taking Charge*, Collins, 1985. It was taken up by the US Army War College.

48. The reality distortion field is well described here: http://www.folklore.org/StoryView.py?project=Macintosh&story=Reality_Distortion_Field.txt&sortOrder=Sort+by+Date.

49. Waters, R. (2016) 'Elon Musk, billionaire tech idealist and space entrepreneur', *Financial Times*, 30 September.

50. Tichy, N.M. and Sherman, S. (2005) *Control Your Destiny or Someone Else Will*. Collins Business Essentials.

51. See my book (2012) *How to Influence and Persuade*. Pearson.

52. Schwarzer, R. and Renner, B. 'Health-Specific Self-Efficacy Scales', available at: https://userpage.fu-berlin.de/health/healself.pdf.

53. Beck, K.H. and Lund, A.K. (1981) 'The effects of health threat seriousness and personal efficacy upon intentions and behavior', *Journal of Applied Social Psychology*, 11, pp. 401–15.

54. Langer, E.J. and Rodin, J. (1976) 'The effects of choice and enhanced personal responsibility for the aged: A field experiment in an institutional setting', *Journal of Personality and Social Psychology*, 34(2), pp. 191–8.

55. *Hamlet*, Act V, Scene ii.

56. William Ernest Henley, 1888.

57. Chadwick, O. (1990) *The Penguin History of the Church: The Reformation: Reformation*. Penguin.

58. A business I've been involved with.
59. I refer to Royal Marines training as both 15 months and 19 months. Acceptance into the Royal Marines normally requires completion of a 4-month pre-joining fitness course, followed by the formal 15-month training course.
60. I have disguised both the individual and the school in this case, at their request. The case was not abnormal in the early years of Teach First.
61. Most of the commentary about the Royal Marine Commandos comes from direct research with them, and I am grateful to Colonel Ken Oliver for his kind help. There is also a good research paper on them: 'The Ethos of the Royal Marines' by Dr Anthony King, University of Exeter, May 2004.
62. See my book (2012) *How to Influence and Persuade*. Pearson.

Chapter 5

63. https://www.thriveglobal.com/stories/29605-in-an-8-hour-day-the-average-worker-is-productive-for-this-many-hours.
64. https://www.workfront.com/resources/2017-2018-state-of-enterprise-work-report-u-s-edition.
65. TQM: total quality management, which is a staple practice of effective manufacturing.
66. https://stireducation.org/.
67. http://thehill.com/homenews/state-watch/326995-census-more-americans-have-college-degrees-than-ever-before.
68. Dempsey, M.A. (1994) 'Fordlandia', *Michigan History*, 78 (4), pp. 24–33.
69. My original research, 1988.
70. https://data.worldbank.org/indicator/NE.TRD.GNFS.ZS. Note that there has been a flattening out of the growth of world trade since the 2009 financial crisis. No one knows if this is a temporary blip or structural shift.
71. Claudius is speaking, in *Hamlet*, Act IV, Scene v.
72. *The Prince* by Nicolo Machiavelli, Chapter XVII, 'Concerning Cruelty and Clemency', and 'Whether It Is Better to Be Loved Than Feared'.
73. *Hamlet*, Act III, Scene i.
74. https://www.health.harvard.edu/mental-health/can-relationships-boost-longevity-and-well-being.
75. https://www.amherst.edu/system/files/media/0759/Brown-Giving-PsychSci-2003.pdf.

76. *The Bible*, Galatians VI.
77. Family firms are not always harmonious. See Gordon, G. and Nicholson, N. (2010) *Family Wars: Stories and Insights from Famous Family Business Feuds*. Kogan Page.
78. Machiavelli, *The Prince*, Chapter XVII.
79. Boggs died in 2017, see: https://news.artnet.com/art-world/jsg-boggs-money-artist-died-62-828554.
80. I wrote 'The Wrong Sort of Money: Options for Quantitative Easing' for Centre Forum in 2013. It questions what the nature of money really is.
81. This was the MAC Group, which had a catastrophic merger with United Research and then with Gemini. It killed a great firm.
82. Chan, E. and Sengupta, J. (2010) 'Insincere Flattery Actually Works: A Dual Attitudes Perspective', *Journal of Marketing Research*, February, Vol. 47, No. 1, pp. 122–33.
83. ACR is a staple of the Positive Psychology movement, which has its roots in work started at the University of Pennsylvania.

Chapter 6

84. The first account of Archimedes in the bath comes from *De Architectura Libri Decem* by Marcus Vitruvius Pollio, Book 9, paragraphs 9–12.
85. The original manuscript of Newton's apple story can now be viewed online (sometimes) through the Royal Society. The BBC provides a link here: http://news.bbc.co.uk/1/hi/sci/tech/8461591.stm. The quotation is from Stukeley's 1752 biography, *Memoirs of Sir Isaac Newton's Life*.
86. Medical students remember the sympathetic division with the four Fs: fight, flight, fright and f**k, although the last 'F' should more accurately be focus.
87. https://www.mayoclinic.org/healthy-lifestyle/adult-health/in-depth/burnout/art-20046642.
88. 'Survey of 614 US HR professionals', conducted by Dana Wilkie of Morar Consulting from 14–19 November 2016, *Society for Human Resource Management*, 31 January 2017.
89. https://www.statista.com/statistics/675233/situations-and-areas-of-life-where-adults-felt-stressed-us/.
90. *Hamlet*, Act III, Scene i, part of the "To be or not to be" speech.
91. Taylor, F.W. (1911) *The Principles of Scientific Management*, Chapter 2, p. 59.
92. Schmidt's real name is reputed to have been Henry Noll.

93. Williamson, A.M. and Feyer, A.M. (2000) 'Moderate sleep deprivation produces impairments in cognitive and motor performance equivalent to legally prescribed levels of alcohol intoxication', *Occupational and Environmental Medicine*, 57: pp. 649–55.
94. OECD data, available at https://data.oecd.org/lprdty/gdp-per-hour-worked.htm.
95. Pilita Clark in *Financial Times*, 6 May 2018.
96. Ninlabs research , available at: http://blog.ninlabs.com/2013/01/programmer-interrupted//.
97. Rubinstein, J.S. and Meyer D.E. (2001), 'Human Perception and Performance', *Journal of Experimental Psychology*, Vol. 27, No. 4.
98. Zerubavel, E. (1989) *The Seven Day Circle: The History and Meaning of the Week*. University of Chicago Press.
99. Lacus Curtius – Roman Calendar – Nundinae (*William Smith's Dictionary of Greek and Roman Antiquities, 1875*).
100. Ker, J. (2010) 'Nundinae: The Culture of the Roman Week', *Phoenix*, Vol. 64, No. 3, *Classical Association of Canada*, pp. 360–85.
101. https://www.royalnavy.mod.uk/careers/royal-marines/get-fit-to-join/my-fitness-plan.
102. https://stats.oecd.org/Index.aspx?DataSetCode=ANHRS.
103. Alhola, P. and Polo-Kantola, P. (2007) 'Sleep Deprivation: Impact on Cognitive Performance', *Neuropsychiatric Disease and Treatment*, 3.5, pp. 553–67.
104. 'Prevalence of Drowsy Driving Crashes: Estimates from a Large-Scale Naturalistic Driving Study', AAA Foundation for Traffic Safety, 2018.
105. Mah, C.D., Mah, K.E., Kezirian, E.J. and Dement, W.C., (2011) 'The Effects of Sleep Extension on the Athletic Performance of Collegiate Basketball Players', *Sleep*, 34(7): pp. 943–50, DOI:10.5665/SLEEP.1132.
106. Londres, A. (1924), 'Les frères Pélissier et leur camarade Ville abandonnent', *Le Petit Parisien*, 27 June.
107. Correa-Burrows, P., Burrows, R., Blanco, E., Reyes, M. and, Gahagan, S, (2016) 'Nutritional quality of diet and academic performance in Chilean students', *Bulletin of the World Health Organization*, 94(3):185–92, DOI:10.2471/BLT.15.161315.
108. Adolphus, K., Lawton, C.L. and Dye, L. (2013) 'The effects of breakfast on behavior and academic performance in children and adolescents', *Frontiers in Human Neuroscience*, 7: p. 425, DOI:10.3389/fnhum.2013.00425.

109. Zainab, T. and Rashed, A.S. (2017) 'The Effect of Breakfast on Academic Performance among High School Students in Abu Dhabi', *Arab Journal of Nutrition and Exercise*, Vol. 2, No. 1, pp. 40–9.

110. Katie Davies, Association of Teachers and Lecturers press release, 19 March 2013.

111. The NHS (June 2016) reviewed the evidence of multiple studies and found that having a proper breakfast may help control weight, but the case is not proven. See: https://www.nhs.uk/news/food-and-diet/should-we-eat-breakfast-like-a-king-and-dinner-like-a-pauper/.

112. Murray, A.D., Daines, L., Archibald, D., et al. (2017) 'The relationships between golf and health: a scoping review', *British Journal of Sports Medicine*, 51:12–19, see: https://bjsm.bmj.com/content/51/1/12.

113. Pereira, A.C., Huddleston, D.E., Brickman, A.M., et al. (2007) 'An in vivo correlate of exercise-induced neurogenesis in the adult dentate gyrus', *Proceedings of the National Academy of Sciences of the United States of America*, 104(13), pp. 5638–43. DOI:10.1073/pnas.0611721104.

114. Erickson, K.I., et al. (2009) 'Aerobic fitness is associated with hippocampal volume in elderly humans', *Hippocampus*, October, 19(10), pp. 1030–9.

115. Heidi Godman, Executive Editor, Harvard Health Blog, Harvard Medical School, 'Regular exercise changes the brain to improve memory, thinking skills', posted 9 April 2014, updated 5 April 2018.

116. Vazou, S. and Smiley-Oyen, A.J. (2014), 'Moving and academic learning are not antagonists: acute effects on executive function and enjoyment', *Sport Exercise Psychology*, October, 36(5), pp. 474–85, DOI: 10.1123/jsep.2014-0035.

117. Bidzan-Bluma, I., and Lipowska, M., (2018) 'Physical Activity and Cognitive Functioning of Children: A Systematic Review', *International Journal of Environmental Research and Public Health*, 15.4, 800, PMC, Web. 20 September.

118. Uses of a paperclip might include DVD drive opener, nail cleaner, small aerial for TV/radio, lock pick, worm hook, ear rings, finger splint, marshmallow sticks, scratching tool (beneath plaster cast) and about 90 others, found here: https://leoniehallatinnovationiq.wordpress.com/2012/11/21/100-uses-for-paperclips/.

119. Oppezzo, M. and Schwartz, D.L. (2014) 'Give your ideas some legs: The positive effect of walking on creative thinking', *Journal of Experimental Psychology: Learning, Memory, and Cognition*, 40(4), pp. 1142–52.

Chapter 7

120. No one is sure where this adage has come from, although it is much used. 'Old adage' is the most reliable and accurate source.
121. Rayner, K ., et al. (2006) 'Raeding Wrods With Jubmled Lettres, There Is a Cost', *Psychological Science*, 17(3), pp. 192–3.
122. Mischel, W., Ebbesen, E.B. and Raskoff Zeiss, A. (1972) 'Cognitive and attentional mechanisms in delay of gratification', *Journal of Personality and Social Psychology*, 21 (2), pp. 204–18.
123. Schlam, T.R. et al. (2013) 'Preschoolers' delay of gratification predicts their body mass 30 years later', *The Journal of Pediatrics*, 162, pp. 90–3.
124. Casey, B.J., et al. (2011) 'Behavioral and neural correlates of delay of gratification 40 years later', *PNAS*, 6 September, 108 (36), pp. 14998–15003.
125. http://health.nzdf.mil.nz/mind/building-mental-resilience/relaxation-and-breathing/.
126. I am deeply grateful to the monks of Wat Suan Mokkh for their course in meditation and breathing.
127. Original interviews.
128. Interview with me.
129. This story was widely reported at the time, including on the BBC, see: https://www.bbc.co.uk/news/world-africa-45611436.
130. There are plenty of examples of desert survival and space survival on the web. Google the terms and find the version you like the most.

Chapter 8

131. https://www.christies.com/features/Hokusai-7458-1.aspx. This is also widely quoted elsewhere.
132. https://inside.6q.io/190-examples-of-company-values/. This lists the corporate values of many top firms.
133. My original survey research, first published in *How to Lead*, Pearson, 2015.
134. Sean Parker has since left Facebook. This interview was first carried by Axios on 9 November 2017 and widely reported across the media, see: https://www.axios.com/sean-parker-unloads-on-facebook-god-only-knows-what-its-doing-to-our-childrens-brains-1513306792-f855e7b4-4e99-4d60-8d51-2775559c2671.html.
135. Brickman, P., Coates, D. and Janoff-Bulman, R. (1978) 'Lottery winners and accident victims: Is happiness relative?', *Journal of Personality and Social Psychology*, 36 (8), pp. 917–27.

136. Lucas, R.E., Clark, A.E., Georgellis, Y. and, Diener, E. (2003) 'Reexamining adaptation and the set point model of happiness: Reactions to changes in marital status', *Journal of Personality and Social Psychology*, 84 (3), pp. 527–39.
137. *The Basic Works of Aristotle*, edited and with an introduction by Richard McKeon, Random House, New York, 1941.
138. Niemiec, C.P., Ryan, R.M. and Deci, E.L. (2009) 'The Path Taken: Consequences of Attaining Intrinsic and Extrinsic Aspirations in Post-College Life', *Journal of Research in Personality*, 73(3): pp. 291–306, DOI:10.1016/j.jrp.2008.09.001.
139. https://www.payscale.com/data-packages/employee-loyalty/full-list.
140. This is standard self-development theory, with the addition of purpose.
141. Wrzesniewski, A., Berg, J.M. and Dutton, J.E. (2010), 'Turn the job you have into the job you want', *Harvard Business Review*, June, pp. 114–17.
142. Frankl, V.E. (2006) *Man's Search for Meaning: An Introduction to Logotherapy*, Beacon Press, Boston, MA (originally published in 1946).
143. Wrzesniewski, A., McCauley, C., Rozin, P. and Schwartz, B. (1997) 'Jobs, Careers, and Callings: People's Relations to Their Work', *Journal of Research in Personality* 31, 21–33, Article No. Rp972162.
144. http://authenticorganizations.com/harquail/2009/12/08/a-job-crafting-example-the-pink-glove-dance/#sthash.lTJsTA19.dpbs.
145. https://www.youtube.com/watch?v=zyq06fuapD0.
146. https://www.payscale.com/data-packages/employee-loyalty/full-list.
147. David was head of risk at RBS from 2013–18 and is now head of risk at another major bank. He had to sort out the mess resulting from the great financial crisis.
148. I was Ian Wrigglesworth's election organiser and saw this event unfold first hand.
149. The Behavioural Insights Team Update Report, 2016–17.
150. http://www.behaviouralinsights.co.uk/wp-content/uploads/2015/07/BIT-Publication-EAST_FA_WEB.pdf.
151. This formed part of a television series on leadership for Teachers TV that I presented.
152. Much else had to change as well: TQM systems, automation, JIT and lean manufacturing, deep training and new ways of using data all had vital roles to play as well in the transformation.
153. Original research, first published in *How to Lead*, Pearson, 2015.

154. Malcolm Gladwell popularised the 10,000 hour rule in *Outliers*, Penguin, 2009.
155. The 10,000 hour rule has been shown to be domain-dependent: it only works in stable, structured environments. See Johansson, F. (2012) 'The Click Moment: Seizing Opportunity in an Unpredictable World', *Portfolio*.
156. My original research, first published in *How to Manage*, Pearson, 2009.

Chapter 9

157. Wyatt, I.D. and Hecker, D.E. (2006), 'Occupational changes during the 20th century', *Monthly Labor Review*, March, available at: https://www.bls.gov/opub/mlr/2006/03/art3full.pdf.
158. Carl Benedikt Frey and Michael Osborne's 'The Future of Employment', available at: https://www.oxfordmartin.ox.ac.uk/downloads/academic/future-of-employment.pdf.
159. Adapted from *How to Manage*, pp. 250–1, Pearson, 2018.
160. Reproduced from *How to Manage*, pp. 246–7, Pearson, 2018.
161. 'Labour Market Statistics: Employment by job tenure intervals: average tenure', OECD Employment and Labour Market Statistics (database), available at: https://doi.org/10.1787/data-00294-en (accessed: 25 August 2018).
162. This fairly brutal assessment came from the head of EMEA at an FMCG firm, who asked to stay anonymous.
163. Phelps' training is recorded consistently across media and events. This one is typical: http://www.borntoworkout.com/michael-phelps-swimming-gym-workout-sets-diet-plan/ . "Up to" 12,000 calories is a debatable claim. No one can take on that many calories every day.
164. From *How to Manage*, pp. 267–8, Pearson, 2018.
165. Dweck, C. (2017) Mindset - Updated Edition: *Changing the Way You Think to Fulfil Your Potential*, 12 January. Robinson.
166. The growth cycle is modelled in Kolb's learning cycle. Sims, R.R. (1983) 'Kolb's Experiential Learning Theory: A Framework for Assessing Person-Job Interaction', *Academy of Management Review*, 8: pp. 501–8. Kolb was inspired by Kurt Lewin, the Gestalt psychotherapist. Kolb's four stages are concrete learning, reflective observation, abstract conceptualisation and active experimentation. Academics like long words.
167. *On The Origin of Species* was published in 1859 and was a sell-out: all 1,250 copies of the first edition were snapped up. But he had

already presented a paper on natural selection to the Linnean Society a year earlier, and no one really noticed how revolutionary it was. You have to sell your achievements: do not assume that everyone will notice for you.

168. See my book *Leadership Skills Handbook*, Kogan Page, 2107.

169. For examples of this 'genius and jerk' formula, see, among others: https://www.cnet.com/news/steve-jobs-an-apt-portrait-of-a-jerk-and-a-genius/, https://www.forbes.com/sites/davidcoursey/2011/10/12/steve-jobs-was-a-jerk-you-shouldnt-be/#6529fa9a4045 and https://www.inc.com/bill-murphy-jr/steve-jobs-was-a-creative-genius-steve-jobs-was-a-total-jerk.html.

170. This remark is also attributed to US department store magnate John Wanamaker, Henry Ford, advertising entrepreneur and guru David Ogilvy and many others. See the WPP annual report 2013, available at: http://sites.wpp.com/annualreports/2013/what-we-think/why-its-time-to-say-goodbye-to-ikthtmisoaiw/.

171. An interview I did, first featured in *Mindset of Success*, Kogan Page, 2018.

172. The training starts with a three-month fitness programme before they formally join the Royal Marines to get recruits to a basic standard. They then go through a formal 15-month programme.

173. The training programme is available online at: https://www.royalnavy.mod.uk/-/media/careers-section-redesign/get-fit-to-join/rm-get-fit-to-join/4857_gftj_preprmc_fitness_plan_pdf_v1.pdf.

174. The Royal Navy publishes limited details online at: https://www.royalnavy.mod.uk/careers/royal-marines/get-fit-to-join/stages-and-standards/royal-marines-commando/basic-training.

175. The Royal Marine Commandos are also referred to as the Marine Commandos, the Royal Marines or simply the Commandos.

Chapter 10

176. 'Slick' Willie Sutton denied saying this to reporter Mitch Ohnstad, who may have made up a good quotation. But Sutton did write: "Why did I rob banks? Because I enjoyed it. I loved it. I was more alive when I was inside a bank, robbing it, than at any other time in my life." From Sutton W. and Linn, E. (1976) *Where the Money Was: The Memoirs of a Bank Robber.* Viking Press, p. 160. Enjoyment of your calling, even robbing banks, is a good starting point for developing mastery and resilience, which Slick Willie had in abundance.

177. A much longer list of successful Old Etonians is available at: https://en.wikipedia.org/wiki/List_of_Old_Etonians_born_in_the_20th_century.

178. My original research. See also 'Biology of Metal: Metal Craftsmanship in Tsubame-Sanjo', an exhibition at Japan House London. 21 September 2018.

179. Porter, M.E. (1998) *Competitive Advantage of Nations*. Free Press.

180. This is based on classic research by Frederick Herzberg, Bernhard Mausner and Barbara B. Snyderman in their book '*The Motivation to Work*. John Wiley, 1959.

181. From HMG prison and probation jobs website, available at: https://prisonandprobationjobs.gov.uk/prison-officer/tips-for-applying/, accessed: 22 February 2019.

182. US Bureau of Labor Statistics January 2018, available at: https://www.bls.gov/news.release/tenure.t04.htm.

183. Schuurman, B.W. (2018) *Becoming a European Homegrown Jihadist: A Multi-Level Analysis of Involvement in the Dutch Hofstad Group, 2002–2005*. Amsterdam University Press.

184. A concise report prepared by the European Commission's Expert Group on Violent Radicalisation, available at: https://biblio.ugent.be/publication/446365/file/6814706.

Index